Helion & Company Limited
Unit 8 Amherst Business Centre
Budbrooke Road
Warwick
CV34 5WE
England
Tel. 01926 499 619
Email: info@helion.co.uk
Website: www.helion.co.uk
Twitter: @helionbooks
Visit our blog http://blog.helion.co.uk/

Published by Helion & Company 2020
Designed and typeset by Farr out Publications, Wokingham, Berkshire
Cover designed by Paul Hewitt, Battlefield Design (www.battlefield-design.co.uk)
Printed by Henry Ling Limited, Dorchester, Dorset

ISBN 978-1-913336-39-4

British Library Cataloguing-in-Publication Data
A catalogue record for this book is available from the British Library

CONTENTS

Notes: To avoid any discussion (and following UN guidelines) about the names of the islands or their locations, their names in both English and Spanish are used. For better understanding of ranks used by the two navies, and while observing that those cited in the book are as at the time of the events, the following table is a list of their equivalents for the Armada Argentina (left column) and the Royal Navy (right column).

Oficiales	Officers	Suboficiales	Ratings
Almirante	Admiral	*Suboficial Mayor*	Warrant Officer
Vicealmirante	Vice Admiral	*Suboficial Principal*	Warrant Officer
Contralmirante	Rear Admiral	*Suboficial Primero*	Chief Petty Officer
Comodoro de Marina	Commodore	*Suboficial Segundo*	Petty Officer
Capitán de Navío	Captain	*Cabo Principal*	Leading Hand
Capitán de Fragata	Commander	*Cabo Primero*	Leading Hand
Capitán de Corbeta	Lieutenant-Commander	*Cabo Segundo*	Able Seaman 1
Teniente de Navío	Lieutenant	*Marinero Primero*	Able Seaman 2
Teniente de Fragata	Sub-Lieutenant	*Marinero Segundo*	New Entry
Teniente de Corbeta	Acting Sub-Lieutenant		
Guardiamarina	Acting Sub-Lieutenant		

As far as the vocabulary is concerned, some technical terms have been used where necessary and hopefully it is not too difficult to follow for the average reader. Likewise, we have tried to minimise the use of acronyms and abbreviations.

Finally, all times used are Zulu (GMT): the sun was rising at approximately 1100 and the sunset was at 1900.

ABBREVIATIONS AND ACRONYMS

AAW	anti-air warfare
ARA	Armada de la República Argentina
ASW	anti-submarine warfare
BRUISER	air launched anti-ship missile
CERTSUB	certain submarine (target classification)
CO	commanding officer
COFUERSUB	Argentina Submarine Force Command
ECM	electronic countermeasures
ESM	electronic support measures
FOSM	Flag Officer Submarines
GPMG	general purpose machine gun
HVU	high value unit
MAD	magnetic anomaly detector
NAS	Naval Air Squadron
NONSUB	no submarine (target classification)
POSSUB	possible submarine (target classification)
PROBSUB	probable submarine (target classification)
RISER	a radar contact which has suddenly appeared
SAU	surface attack unit
SINKER	a radar contact that later disappeared
TF	task force
TF	task group
WOLF	visually identified surfaced hostile submarine

FOREWORD

This is a wonderful work.

Its lessons are also magnificent.

When Mariano enquired as to whether I would be interested in writing the foreword for the book, a certain ethical objection went before me. I only knew a small part of this story, therefore... should I do it? Should I present myself? What could I say?

After having read it and facing the enormous magnitude of this symphony of men without voices or means, my objections faded into the background. Therefore, I accepted the task with pleasure.

With his usual humble prudence, Mariano made the remark that the contents of this book were not for the study and analysis of the military. However, I would disagree with this. On the contrary, it is particularly rich in so many aspects that – from seasoned naval analysts to newly initiated students – they would be able to draw valuable conclusions regarding this aspect of war at sea. This is, for those who really want to extract them.

In the reading of the first lines of this is the primary lesson of the whole story: the effort that must be taken by a force, with an imposing anti-submarine capability in the face of a small but not insignificant submarine threat. Such an effort – necessary, methodical, efficient and maintained until the end of the conflict – was an out of proportion force against a couple of submarines, one of them very antiquated indeed, besides the serious limitations forced upon them due to their maintenance and operational readiness.

The quantity of munitions used; the huge amount of fuel burned and toll on machinery; the hard exertions – both physical and mental – imposed on the crews due to the permanent anti-torpedo measures; and finally the limitations of operations of the Task Force – despite the open help from the US Navy and the help gained from the deciphering of Argentine communications – speak of the complexity they had to face.

Isn't there anything to learn from this?

The British force was aided by the United States, we were only helped by the whales.

My father was a submariner and I followed in his footsteps with the conviction that the submarine was the real answer to the needs of the defence of the sea within our national objectives. Today, in my old age, this conviction is more necessary than ever: my own experiences taught me that.

Unfortunately, this belief is not shared by most of my colleagues who continue to cling to, in my view, out of date visions regarding the composition of a naval power which is not compatible with the economic resources of Argentina.

Today, the degree of uncertainty in the structure of a modern military power is directly related to the speed of technological advances. So, a force that now seems very effective can become obsolete in a very short time.

In that sense, I am sure that the submarine will continue to be a great deterrent in the coming decades. Their destructive capacity has increase exponentially with the ability to launch submarine-to-air and submarine-to-ship missiles in addition to the reduction in noise, and propulsion systems which don't require air and which has made them much more covert and elusive.

The war at sea does not appear to be as fierce or bloody as combat on land where two enemies, filled with hate and furore, engage in body to body combat. In the majority of cases, at sea, the enemy is, or might be, just a blip on a screen or a noise that has been detected. Although the heart speeds up when these are detected, it is difficult to hate such things.

However, war at sea is absolutely brutal, with weapons that penetrate steel and destroy men. It is driven, at all times, with a cold and lethal professionalism.

The deaths in this conflict, both military and civilian, corroborates it. 54.8% of the Argentine losses were at sea (90% of which, and 49.6% of the total, came from the sinking of the cruiser ARA *General Belgrano*). 57.6% of the British losses came on board ships as a result of attacks by aircraft or land-based missiles.

Therefore, I bow my head as a mark of respect and honour to all of those who fought for their courage and sacrifice, on either side, in the cold and cruel waters of the South Atlantic.

I hold no grudges in my spirit, only pain for fallen companions whose effort was not enough to prevent the loss of these islands. Although I believe the cause our enemy was fighting for was not a just one, they, as servicemen, fulfilled their duty with determination and professionalism and I cannot reproach them for it.

As for the Argentine submariners, his was, in many cases, an almost desperate professionalism. This is also a tribute to the crew of the submarine ARA *San Luis* for their ability, sacrifice and dedication to their duty.

Always, whenever I think of any of them, the words of the epic Spanish poem *"Cantar de los cantares"* comes to mind, which was recited by the people who saw El Cid and his entourage go into exile: *"God, what a good vassal, if only he had a good lord."*

It was an honour to have commanded them.

Within the pages of this book, some of these thoughts take on a dimension of reality. As I put forward at the beginning;

This is a work of magnificence. Its lessons are also magnificent.

Fernando María Azcueta
Capitán de Navío (RE)
Former commander of the submarine ARA *San Luis* – 1982

INTRODUCTION

This is the story of an episode of modern warfare that involved hundreds of sailors and airmen; dozens of war machines (aircraft, helicopters, ships and submarines) and a large number of weapons used against an enemy - ranging from shots fired from a machine gun to torpedoes with enough explosive power to sink a ship or submarine.

Its participants possessed a high level of advanced training, being true professionals in modern naval warfare. It is also a story of rigid doctrines being adapted to suit new situations, which involved problems that nobody had previously considered and for which solutions had to be found without any delay. It also included some of the most modern weapons available at the time.

It is a story that really should already have been on paper in black and white. However, so far, nobody has written a comprehensive account about the anti-submarine war in the South Atlantic.

Prior to 2019, the only things to have been written about this subject were some short articles which really are just fragments of the full story. This changed with the publication of *A Carrier at Risk*, published by Helion that year.

That book detailed the Argentine's Navy anti-submarine assets and their efforts to protect the only Argentine aircraft carrier, the *25 de Mayo*, from the British submarines that were trying to sink it, while it withdrew from the conflict zone to the presumed safe coastal waters.

This second book is almost the inverse history of *A Carrier at Risk* in as much as the submarines would be Argentine instead of British, and those who were trying to sink them would be British and not the Argentines.

There must have been some good reasons that such a fascinating subject has never been put on paper prior to these books. I personally believe that there were two reasons, or at least two main ones.

The first is that the anti-submarine war does not appear to be as interesting as events that took place during the 1982 conflict. A quick review of the subject would conclude that the Argentine submarines did not sink any British ships and that the British anti-submarine effort was unable to track down the only submarine operational in the conflict zone around the islands, the ARA *San Luis*, and only managed to damage and disable the ARA *Santa Fe*, which was on a resupply mission to South Georgia (Georgias del Sur). Therefore, it would seem that nothing of any relevance happened.

Obviously, it was not like this, as we shall see.

The second one is that everything relating to submarines and how to destroy them was a jealously guarded secret that needed to be maintained. Until as recently as 2017 there were no declassified documents (in the UK or in Argentina) that would allow a book to be written on the subject, bearing in mind that oral accounts only enable partial recreation of such precise events.

On a personal level, the submarine and anti-submarine warfare has always been of great interest to me, possibly since reading *U-Boat 977* by Heinz Schäffer. This is the fascinating tale of the voyage undertaken by a German U-Boat to the Argentine submarine base of Mar del Plata following the surrender of Germany in the Second World War. In addition, having studied the Falklands/Malvinas war over the years, I now possess a large collection of books and articles and have had access to many documents in both the British National Archives and the Argentine Naval Archive on the subject.

I finally made the decision to write this book following a long chat over a cup of tea with *Capitán de Navío* (Retired) Fernando Azcueta, the commander of the Argentine Type 209 submarine ARA *San Luis* during the conflict. While listening attentively to his account of being a submarine commander, carrying out attacks and being attacked, I realised that this was a story that merited being told. The result is this book.

Fortunately, in this story, no vessels were sunk and many of the protagonists of the tale collaborated in the task of putting the complete narrative together. Some of them were happy to be credited (and they are mentioned both in the text and as credits to the photos) while others wished to remain anonymous. A further result of the process of researching the book was that I had the great satisfaction of being able to put former enemies in touch with one another.

It is not a complete story of the conflict, nor the naval war. It is simply an account of the British part of the anti-submarine operations that took place. In addition, it also includes accounts of operations undertaken by Argentine submarines during the conflict that have not been written about anywhere else. It would be true to say that a complete story of the Argentine submarine force's actions during the conflict is yet to be written.

This is a history book, not a book about naval tactics for a military college, therefore the language used tries to explain step by step what occurred for the average reader. That said, the questions that are often tackled are extremely detailed and technical in nature. It is difficult to give an explanation of modern naval warfare without passing over that line.

I hope that this will be a fitting recognition of the combatants of both sides: members of the Argentine Navy, the Royal Navy and the Royal Air Force, who took part in the tense struggle either above or below the waves in the cold waters of the South Atlantic. All of them carried out their duty and all, to a greater or lesser extent, completed their assigned missions. They should feel proud of themselves.

This book is dedicated to my family, my wife Natasha and my children: Lola, Tomás and Lucas.

I also want to thank my friends Alejandro Amendolara, Andrea Assanelli, Pablo Castro, David Lagar, Daniel Mesa (a friend and webmaster of the wonderful ElSnorkel.com -www.elsnorkel.com - the best web page about South American submarines), Javier Ruberto (who also wants to thank Andrés Cieslinski, Pablo M. Gonzales, Ariel Pelayo, Rodrigo Barraza and Pablo P. Albornoz), Chris Herbert, Gorka L Martínez Mezo and many others. A special thanks is reserved for Andy Smith given that without his help and collaboration this book would not have been possible.

1
SUPERB WENT NORTH

During the final days of March 1982, a nuclear-powered submarine was detected in the Western Approaches (the rectangular maritime area to the west of the British Isles). It is possible that it had been picked up by SOSUS (Sound Surveillance System – the network of hydrophones on the seabed operated by NATO in order to detect submarines) and this had triggered an alert of a possible intruder that had breached the Greenland-Iceland-UK gap (known as the "GIUK gap"), had entered the Atlantic Ocean and then headed south.

The Royal Navy's Swiftsure-class nuclear-powered attack submarine, HMS *Superb*, was the alert boat and therefore responsible for dealing with submerged intruders near British waters.

Under the command of Commander James Perowne, it had just arrived in Gibraltar on 26 March, where it was due to spend five days involved in the series of exercises that were taking place in the area (collaborating in the anti-submarine warfare drills) called SPRINGTRAIN 82.

As Perowne recalls: "I was handed a signal telling me to sail forthwith as a Soviet submarine had penetrated the Northern Fleet Exercise Areas". So, he informed the crew that they had to quickly cancel their reservations in the hotels of The Rock. Hours later, *Superb* set sail from Gibraltar. From there, it headed north towards the Rockall Bank in order to carry out Operation Sardius. It was a long way from a developing crisis in South Georgia.

Finally, it found the intruder, a Soviet nuclear-powered attack submarine, possibly a Project 671RT *Syomga* (NATO reporting name Victor II) class boat. *Superb* trailed it for several days and monitored all its movements. "We have a Russian problem", Roger Lane-Nott, commander of HMS *Splendid* (a sister ship of *Superb*), was slightly surprised on hearing the news having scarcely set foot in the naval base´s operations room. Yet another submarine had been detected in the Western Approaches. HMS *Splendid*'s orders were to depart immediately from its base in Faslane, in the Firth of Clyde, locate the submarine and then covertly follow it.

The appearance of the new intruder coincided with the arrival of a Soviet Primorye-class intelligence-gathering ship off the Hebrides. This ship, the 4,500-tonne displacement *Zaporozhye* (CER-501), was under the command of Captain 1st Class P. Zyryanov.

Two of the seven available British nuclear-powered hunter-killer submarines were tasked to deal with Soviet intrusions. It was never comfortable for the Royal Navy to have submarine intruders so close to some of their main naval bases.

A short time later, the second unwanted guest was located by HMS *Splendid* and identified by its acoustic signature as being a Soviet Victor III (Project 671RTM/RTMK *Shchuka*) class submarine. This nuclear-powered hunter-killer submarine had only recently been introduced to the Soviet Navy and was the pride of the submarine fleet.

HMS *Superb* with the Rock of Gibraltar in the background. (Royal Navy)

A Soviet Victor III-class nuclear-powered attack submarine underway on the surface. (US Navy)

As Jonathon "Jonty" Powis, a member of the nuclear submarine HMS *Conqueror*'s crew during the Falklands/Malvinas conflict, recalled: "Until the mid-80s UK and US attack submarines had a strong advantage over the Soviet subs in signature (Soviet ones were very noisy) and sensors (the UK/US towed array). The Soviet Victor III was the first of their boats to begin to match us for signature."

Nevertheless, on the afternoon of 29 March, a VLF transmission picked up by *Splendid* obliged Lane-Nott to return to periscope depth in order to receive a ciphered message which informed him about the escalation of the situation in the South Atlantic and the requirement to return to port, to resupply for a new mission there. It was with a certain reluctance that Lane-Nott ordered contact with the Soviet submarine to be broken off and to return to Faslane. The commander considered that this had been a particularly challenging hunt. It would be left to other units, particularly those of the RAF, to pick up the tracking of the Victor III submarine.

This would not be the first intruder of the year that the Nimrod MR2s of 18 Group, based in Kinloss and St Mawgan, would be asked to deal with. In fact, this would be the seventh Operation Oedipus to be carried out that year. Oedipus was the codeword for operations to track Soviet submarines. For the crews, these operations were somewhat more interesting than the usual Operation Tapestry missions which deal with monitoring fishing boats. According to the then current doctrines, the large four-engine specialist anti-submarine aircraft would commence sowing passive omnidirectional sonobuoy barriers across the projected route being taken by the intruder.

The first fruits of their labours came on 1 April when a solid contact was made in the early hours of the morning. Further LOFAR (omnidirectional passive sonar) and DIFAR (directional) sonobuoys were laid and it was determined that this contact could be the submarine that had been stalked by HMS *Splendid*.

At 0900, once another Nimrod had taken over the role of monitoring the field of sonobuoys, the intruder briefly exposed its fin (otherwise known as its sail), which raised the category of the contact to

Periscope view of RAF Nimrod MR2 XV232, taken from Argentine submarine ARA *Santa Cruz* in November 1984. The submarine was in the English Channel, travelling from Germany (where it was built) to Argentina. (Juan Ignacio Rela)

A Lynx HAS.2 helicopter aboard HMS *Invincible* (R05) during FLEET EX 1-90. (US Navy)

CERTSUB. As Joe Kennedy, then a young crew member onboard the aircraft, recalled:

> Halfway through the flight came the unforgettable and confident call, "Captain, radar, RISER, bearing 070, 11 miles". The captain called the crew to action stations and everyone reacted like a well-oiled machine, setting up for first pass photography, preparing to monitor active buoys, manning ordnance and generally being prepared for immediate action.
>
> What was really unusual though was that the tail was hanging out of the water at an angle of about 30° with the multi-bladed prop spinning wildly in mid air…the conning tower eventually started sinking out of danger, but not before a magazine of film had been shot, capturing the whole sorry tale of the planesman's desperation to get the boat back beneath the waves.

The submarine, now aware it had been detected, turned to the north and maintained a depth of 500 fathoms (3,000 feet). The contact was definitively lost during the early evening and was not re-established by any of the three following sorties.

Also taking part in the operation were Royal Navy Sea King anti-submarine helicopters of both 819 and 824 Naval Air Squadrons.

The hunt proved to be very successful. The coordinated British units operating in a known environment had successfully carried out all phases of anti-submarine warfare: detection, localisation, classification and pursuit. As a summary, following the initial detection by SOSUS, two nuclear-powered submarines were sent to follow the intruders and then the role was passed to the RAF Nimrod fleet with further collaboration from the Royal Navy helicopters. One of the enemy submarines was even harassed until it had left the area. Prior to the break off, it had been photographed, much to the humiliation of its captain.

The Soviet boats were identified by their acoustic signatures, it was known where there were operating from and their technical and human limitations were common knowledge within the British (and NATO) ASW specialists. In 1982, the Royal Navy was considered to be the anti-submarine warfare specialist within NATO (North Atlantic Treaty Organisation). It possessed highly trained personnel and the required technical resources with which to face the threat of the Soviet submarines in the North Atlantic.

At the beginning of the 1980s, about 50 percent of all anti-submarine operations in the Eastern Atlantic were carried out by the Royal Navy. The Royal Navy's focus of operations was anti-submarine warfare. This is as was set out by the then Under-Secretary of State for Defence for the Royal Navy (Mr. Keith Speed) to the House of Commons on 19 June 1980:

> The main maritime threat to the Alliance in the Atlantic comes from the Soviet Northern Fleet based on the Kola peninsula, particularly its powerful nuclear-powered submarine force, and maritime power is essential to the success of the Alliance's strategy of deterrence. It is to counter this threat that the Royal Navy of today is primarily oriented towards anti-submarine warfare.

Obviously, it is important not to forget the degree of collaboration and coordination that was taking place between the Royal Navy and the US Navy. In certain areas, such as anti-submarine warfare, everything was shared between the navies of both countries. This was,

A Royal Navy Westland Sea King HAS.5 flies alongside US Navy aircraft carrier USS *Nimitz* (CVN-68) during NATO Exercise NORTHERN WEDDING 86. (US Navy)

A Mk 46 torpedo being released from a US Navy SH-3 Sea King, during exercises in 1977. (US Navy)

of course, entirely logical given that they were both key members of the same alliance.

The main antagonist of NATO´s ACLANT (Allied Command Atlantic, based at the Norfolk Naval Base in the US) during the Cold War was the Soviet Navy (Voyenno-morskoy flot SSSR) and its fleet of submarines. The main Soviet threat came from beneath the waves as the Soviet surface fleet was no match for the forces of NATO. The 1981-82 edition of *Jane's Fighting Ships* puts the Soviet submarine fleet size at 156 ballistic or cruise missile submarines, 50 nuclear-powered hunter-killer submarines and 160 conventional (Diesel / Electric) attack submarines. Of interest to NATO's Command in the North Atlantic was that these submarines could be assigned to either the Northern Fleet, Baltic Fleet or Black Sea Fleet, the first mentioned being the most powerful and the only one that had nuclear-powered submarines in its inventory.

However, the operations that took place in the South Atlantic in 1982 were of a completely different nature to the role that the Royal Navy (and Royal Air Force) had been training for. The submarine threat would be present there, but the submarines would not be noisy Soviet ones; nor would the US Navy be there to help with its Carrier Groups; there would not be any SOSUS system to help detect targets; the Air Force would not be near and the area of operations was almost completely unknown.

ACLANT and its anti-submarine assets were very far away.

2
SUPERB WENT SOUTH

The plans to retake the Malvinas (or invade the Falkland Islands depending on your point of view) had been sitting in files within the Military Junta that had been governing Argentina, since the end of 1981. The idea was to have a military plan in case of the failure of the diplomatic negotiations that were being held from the beginning of 1982. Since 1965, the United Nations had been urging that the two parties find a peaceful solution to the sovereignty dispute that had existed almost since the islands had been discovered. However, the reality was that no satisfactory progress, in the eyes of the Junta, was being made in these negotiations.

The belief within the Junta was that that they would be able to occupy the islands without spilling any blood, and once established there, their negotiating position would dramatically improve:

> The recovery of the Islands would not have the purpose of conflict´s escalation, nor end the negotiations or replace them, since escalation was not the most acceptable measure for achieving the political objective. On the contrary, it was intended to start a serious and substantive negotiation.

Obviously, this plan counted on the UK not responding militarily and the United States maintaining its neutrality regarding the sovereignty of the islands. It would be an almost entirely naval operation in nature and therefore the responsibility of the Argentine Navy and its head, *Almirante* Jorge Isaac Anaya, also a member of the ruling Junta (along with the Army and Air Force counterparts) After all, it seemed, the islands that were near Argentina, and to the extreme south of the American continent, were not now relevant. Or, at least, that was the reading the Military Junta had given to the "hints" from London.

The Argentine plans envisaged that the earliest date that the operation could take place would be 15 May 1982. The Royal Navy, about to suffer significant cuts to their allocation of the British defence budget, would by then have had a significant reduction in the number of ships available to them. However, events took over the plans during March that year.

Workers hired by Argentine businessman Constantino Davidoff, who had been granted a contract to reduce the former whaling stations on South Georgia (Georgias del Sur) to scrap metal, had raised the Argentine flag having barely landed on the island, on 19 March, which was considered to be a provocation by the United Kingdom. This event caused HMS *Endurance*, the Royal Navy's main presence in Antarctica and the Falklands/Malvinas during the Austral summer, to be sent from Port Stanley to remove them. The Argentine Navy, in turn, sent two corvettes and a logistics ship to the area to intercept *Endurance* and prevent this from happening.

In the midst of the developing crisis, HMS *Superb* had sailed from Gibraltar, as already mentioned, in order to begin its hunt for the Soviet submarine intruder. However, the hurried departure was witnessed by the ITN Defence Correspondent, Geoffrey Archer, and was reported on the television channel as being related to what was happening in South Georgia. In other words, it was reported to be heading south, not north.

This information rapidly came to the attention of the Argentine leadership via a secret cable from the Argentine Embassy in London (which clearly had a TV set). In fact, this message relayed the information that two submarines, not one, had set sail in the direction of the South Atlantic. Therefore, it was now or never. According to Anaya:

> The British would reach military superiority when the first ships of its naval force arrived, that is, the first nuclear submarine. According to our calculations it would happen from 10 April. This unfavourable modification of the balance of forces … would not

HMS *Endurance* (A171) and one of its Wasp HAS.1 helicopter in 1979. (MoD)

make military recovery feasible, so this date, 10 April, was the end of the period during which we could operate successfully.

As the negotiations at the United Nations were not making any progress towards the Argentine goal, the reasoning within the Military Junta was that if there were British submarines patrolling the South Atlantic it would not be possible to carry out the operation to capture the islands for the Argentines. Therefore, a green light was given to bring the operation forward.

An amphibious assault was launched (called Operation Rosario) and Argentine troops landed on the islands on 2 April. The Argentine submarine ARA *Santa Fe* took part in the operation by disembarking special forces. The next day, Argentine troops also landed in South Georgia (Georgias del Sur).

A short time later, UK Prime Minister Margaret Thatcher, not being aware of the assumptions that the Junta had made, ordered the formation of a powerful Task Force centred around the aircraft carriers HMS *Hermes* and HMS *Invincible*. Its mission would be to restore British sovereignty to all the territories that had been captured by the Argentines.

3
THE SUBMARINE THREAT

Like any naval force, the Task Force was exposed to air, surface and submarine threats. The Royal Navy considered the Argentine submarine force to be a serious and credible threat to the British Task Force. Therefore, from the start of the conflict, steps were taken to ensure the anti-submarine protection of the fleet, especially the Carrier Battle Group (Task Group 317.8).

Whilst the British Task Force was sailing south, the scant knowledge about the Argentine submarine force was being rapidly updated, as were the plans to neutralise them. The submarine threat was rapidly evaluated by the Royal Navy as consisting of two Second World War era submarines of US origin (ARA *Santa Fe* and ARA *Santiago del Estero* – although the operational capacity of the latter was in some

The British armada – some of the escorts of the Task Force. (Royal Navy)

Submarine ARA *Salta* returning to its home base, from a 50-day patrol, in 1975. This patrol was carried out to test the limits of the submarine and its crew. (Juan Ignacio Rela)

doubt) and two modern German-made Type 209 submarines (ARA *Salta* and ARA *San Luis*). It was not necessary to look very far to discover this information, just picking up a copy of *Jane's Fighting Ships* would bring you to this same conclusion.

In more detail, it was thought that the old US-made submarines would have to penetrate the defensive anti-submarine screen (the anti-submarine assets that protected the main naval units) to be able to use their straight-running Mk 14 torpedoes or even the guided Mk 37 ones given their slow speed, poor precision and short range. A near impossible task for the old and noisy boats.

However, it was considered that the main danger came from the Type 209 submarines and their SST-4 torpedoes. These submarines, according to intelligence reports, presented "a significant threat to surface units of the Task Group 317.8....they are very manoeuvrable, and their main motors are very quiet."

As stated by Commander Chris Craig, CO of the Type 21 Frigate HMS *Alacrity*:

> The formation of a UK Task Group to sail 8,000 miles south to recover the Falkland Islands was optimized to cope with the known threats from Argentinian Forces. Whilst the risk from the air was generally deemed to be our major foe, there was little complacency about the threat from below the waves. The relatively small, silent diesel/electric German-built Type 209 submarines were assessed to be a significant threat, particularly as the bulk of RN ASW training had, for many Cold War years, been optimized against generally larger and oft louder Soviet submarines. The possibility of fighting an inshore battle, most suitable for these quiet conventional subs, had rarely been even war-gamed, as it was deemed as most unlikely. Nevertheless, by necessity, much ASW training and work-up time had still been spent in relatively shallow, coastal areas. Hence, the RN command and sonar teams were much on their guard against Argentinian submarine attack – particularly in the likely focal points of our battle plan (such as our re-provisioning staging point of Ascension, South Georgia and, ultimately, around our intended landing points on the Falklands themselves).

It was also added that, except when snorkelling (which was when the submarine came up to just below the surface and raised its snorkel, to be able to start the noisy diesel engines in order to recharge its batteries), it would be very difficult to detect these submarines with either passive sonobuoys or towed sonar.

The recent British experience against comparable submarines, in the ALLOY EXPRESS exercise which had taken place off the Norwegian coast, had demonstrated that these were "an extremely elusive and difficult target to detect and prosecute" in the opinion of the commander of 820 Naval Air Squadron which operated the latest Sea King anti-submarine helicopters. Likewise, the Royal Navy had gained knowledge of exercises carried out between nuclear-powered submarines of the US Navy and the Argentine Type 209s which often ended in victories for the Argentine Navy.

A modern conventional submarine is much quieter than a nuclear-powered submarine when operating with its main (electric) motors (as, at least during the early 80s, the nuclear reactors required noisy pumps that helped to keep the reactor cool) as well as being much smaller, which was another factor in their favour.

Unaware of the British concerns, the Argentine Navy prepared its submarines to be deployed for the forthcoming war. Chief of Naval Operations *Vice Admiral* Juan José Lombardo, designated TOAS (Teatro de Operaciones del Atlántico Sur or South Atlantic Theatre of Operations) commander, and an experienced submariner, had correctly reasoned that a conventional diesel/electric submarine could

ARA *Santa Fe* and ARA *Santiago del Estero* at their home base (Base Naval Mar del Plata). Mar del Plata Golf Club's courses are clearly visible in the background. The fear during the war was that there might be spies amongst the golfers, so the submarine movements to and from the base were restricted to night hours. (Armada Argentina)

The decommissioned ARA *Santiago del Estero* (former USS *Chivo*) entering the main Argentine Naval Base (Puerto Belgrano) in the early morning light, after its voyage from Mar del Plata. The idea behind this movement was to hide the submarine in this base in order to mislead British intelligence services. (Andrés Feduzi)

not safely actively seek an encounter with the enemy but would be better to patrol an area and to wait for them there.

In fact, whether a submarine is in an offensive or defensive role determines its indiscretion rate: the percentage of time a conventional submarine must spend at periscope depth (to run the diesel engines via the snorkel). During this time a submarine is more vulnerable as it is much easier to detect either its deployed masts while snorkelling (when snorkelling, the periscope, radio mast and ESM mast are usually raised) or from the noise the diesel engines generate.

When on an offensive mission, a submarine must travel further and faster and therefore snorkel more frequently than would be required by a submarine defending a predetermined area. Furthermore, being indiscrete was not an option in the face of the most experienced ASW force in the world. For example, the indiscretion rate for submarine ARA *San Luis* was 34% (34% of the time was snorkelling) when in transit to the operation´s area, but just 12% when in the ENRIQUETA waiting area.

With this in mind, Lombardo´s staff selected three large patrol areas for the Argentine submarines: around South Georgia (Georgias del Sur), near Ascension Island, and in the proximity of the Falklands/Malvinas.

COFUERSUB (a subordinate command) was then ordered to follow the planning of his staff. Indeed, the commander of the Argentine submarine force (COFUERSUB for *Comandante de la Fuerza de Submarinos*), who at the time was *Capitán de Navío* Eulogio Moya Latrubesse, issued on 10 April the secret order COFUERSUB 02 "S"/82 for the *Salta*, *San Luis* and *Santa Fe* (and excluded, as the Royal Navy suspected, the *Santiago del Estero*).

The mission given to the submarine force was finally to: "disrupt the enemy Expeditionary Force in the Malvinas and South Georgia area, with the aim of maintaining and consolidating the retaking of the "ISLAS MALVINAS", indicating that the mission would be achieved by sinking "enemy targets by torpedoes, carried out from patrol areas in the Malvinas and South Georgia as assigned" (Ascension Island, following Lombardo´s orders, was also considered as a patrol area, but it was ruled out for two reasons: the distance involved and, also, because the Argentine Navy did not want to fire the first shots).

The mission of the Argentine submarines was considered to be a defensive one from a strategic point of view (as its aim was to maintain possession of the lands that had been gained) but offensive from a tactical view as it involved attempting to sink enemy ships.

ARA *Santiago del Estero* and ARA *Salta*

At the time of the start of the crisis with the UK, the ARA *Santiago del Estero* (S-22) was not in active service; lacked its sonar (it had been installed in its sister *Santa Fe* following an accident to the latter); deprived of batteries and without the ability to submerge.

It had started life as the USS *Chivo*, launched in 1945, and had been modernised to a Guppy IA standard in 1950 (Guppy stood for "Greater Underwater Propulsion Power Program" which was a program to improve the submerged speed, manoeuvrability and

Table 1: Argentine submarine force in 1982

Submarine	Pennant number	Argentine Navy four-digit code	Class	Accepted into service	Displacement submerged (Tonnes)	Armament	Torpedoes carried during the war	Days on patrol
ARA *San Luis*	S-32	SUSL	Type 209	1974	1,248	8 x bow 533mm torpedo tubes	SST- 4 / Mk 37 mod 3	11 April / 19 May
ARA *Salta*	S-31	SUSA	Type 209	1974	1,248	8 x bow 533mm torpedo tubes	SST- 4 / Mk 37 mod 3	N/A
ARA *Santa Fe*	S-21	SUSF	Balao / Guppy II	1944 (1971 Argentine Navy)	2,440	10 x 533 mm torpedo tubes (6 forward & 4 aft)	Mk 14 / Mk 37 mod 3	16 April / 25 April (2nd patrol)
ARA *Santiago del Estero*	S-22	SUSE	Balao / Guppy IA	1945 (1971 Argentine Navy)	2,440	10 x 533 mm torpedo tubes (6 forward & 4 aft)	N/A	N/A

Sanitized Copy Approved for Release 2010/06/10 : CIA-RDP82T00709R000100940001-3

SECRET

25X1

(c) NATIONAL PHOTOGRAPHIC INTERPRETATION CENTER

Page 1 of 1

Copy____

Attachment to Z-15230/82
NPIC/IEG (S/82)
28 MAY 1982

ARGENTINE NAVAL COMBATANTS
PUERTO BELGRANO NAVAL BASE AND SHIPYARD, ARGENTINA

25X1

1. (S/D) SIGNIFICANCE: MAJOR ARGENTINE NAVAL COMBATANTS AT PUERTO BELGRANO.

2. (S/D) REMARKS: MAJOR VESSELS OF THE ARGENTINE FLEET WERE AT PUERTO BELGRANO NAVAL BASE AND SHIPYARD (GRAPHIC 1 OF 4). VESSELS PRESENT INCLUDED THE 25 DE MAYO AIRCRAFT CARRIER (CV) WITH NO AIRCRAFT ON THE FLIGHT-DECK (GRAPHIC 2 OF 4), ONE GUPPY-CLASS ATTACK SUBMARINE (SS) (GRAPHIC 3 OF 4), ONE TYPE 209-CLASS ATTACK SUBMARINE (SS) IN DRYDOCK (FIGURE 4 OF 4), ONE TYPE-42 GUIDED MISSILE DESTROYER-HELICOPTER (DDGH), ONE GEARING-CLASS FRAM II GUIDED MISSILE DESTROYER (DDG), ONE SUMNER-CLASS DESTROYER (DD), ONE FRENCH TYPE A-69 LIGHT FRIGATE (FFG), FIVE TON-CLASS COASTAL MINESWEEPERS (MSC), AND NUMEROUS AUXILIARIES. 25X1

(S/D) THE OPERATIONAL STATUS OF THE GUPPY SS COULD NOT BE DETERMINED. 25X1

3. (S) COORDINATES 38-53-33S 062-06-16W. 25X1

Analysis of imagery taken by a US KH-11 satellite at the end of May 1982. The NPIC (National Photographic Interpretation Center) analyst reports about the warships in the Puerto Belgrano Naval Base, including a Guppy submarine and a Type 209 submarine, the latter in dry dock. The Guppy was the *Santiago del Estero* and the 209 was the *San Luis*. (US Central Intelligence Agency)

endurance of US Navy submarines). On 1 July 1971 the US Navy handed over the submarine to Argentina and, by 1982, it should have been in a museum.

Its only involvement in the conflict happened on late April, when it moved from the naval base at Mar del Plata to Puerto Belgrano under its own power and with a skeleton crew. Once there, it was hidden between two other ships. The intention was to fool the British forces into thinking that the submarine was elsewhere on operations. However, its hiding place was discovered towards the end of May by a US KH-11 satellite, which put an end to this ruse.

The ARA *Salta* (S-31) was one of the Argentine Navy's two modern Type 209 submarines, known as the Salta-class within the Argentine Navy. The other submarine in this class was the ARA *San Luis* (S-32). The 209s had been ordered in 1968 and, starting in the latter half of 1969, had been built in sections by Howaldtswerke Deutsche Werft (HDW) AG in Kiel, West Germany. The individual sections were then shipped to Argentina for assembly at Tandanor, Buenos Aires, and the two submarines were finally commissioned in 1974.

IKL Industries of Lubeck was responsible for the design of the Type 209-class, which was based on units of smaller displacement (around 450 tons submerged) corresponding to the older Type 205-class that had been constructed for the Bundesmarine (the then West Germany Navy).

The first orders for the Type 209 came from Greece, who ordered four of them, and then Argentina. The Argentine 209s displaced some 1,200 tons submerged, which was slightly more than their Greek counterparts. The acquisition, assembly and operation of the new IKL 209/1200s submarines represented a qualitative jump for the Argentine Navy, which, until the date of their acquisition, had only operated the older Guppy submarines which were by then entering the final phases of their life spans. The Guppies would later be replaced by the Santa Cruz (TR 1700) class of submarines that were being constructed in West Germany at that time of the conflict.

Type 209 submarine ARA *Salta* running on the surface near its home base, Base Naval Mar del Plata (BNMP), 400 km south of Buenos Aires. (Armada Argentina)

The Argentine 209s were 61 metres long and had a maximum surface speed of 11 knots and 21 knots while submerged. They had a range of 8,200 nautical miles and a maximum submerged range (without having to recharge their batteries) of 400 nautical miles when travelling at maximum economy speed of 4 knots. The maximum dive depth was around 250 metres (820 feet).

The class had been fitted with an Atlas AN-525 A6 passive sonar, which was optimised for use in shallow waters and an Atlas AN-407 A9 active sonar and not the improved Krupp-Atlas CSU 3-2 that several reports indicate. The active/passive sonar suite was further enhanced by the fitting of a French Thomson Sintra

A close view of ARA *Salta*'s torpedo tube caps. (Martín Otero)

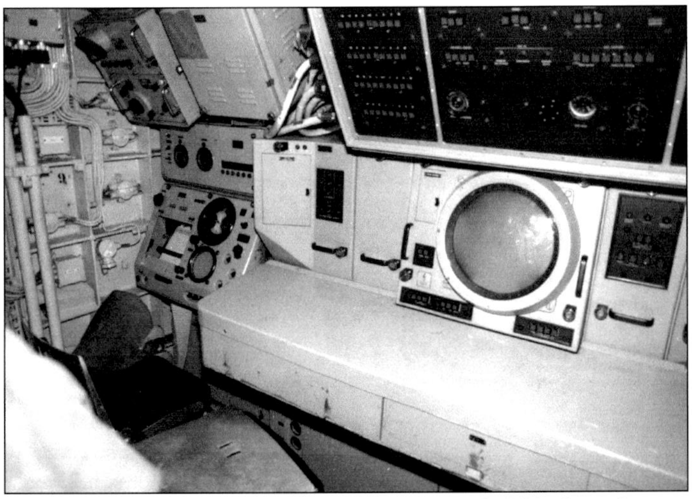

ARA *San Luis'* Control Room: Thomson Sintra DUUX-2C passive range-finding sonar display (extreme left) and above it, the AUUD-1B Interceptor-Analyser console. To the right, the Signaal VM8/24 Fire Control Computer. (via Fernando Azcueta)

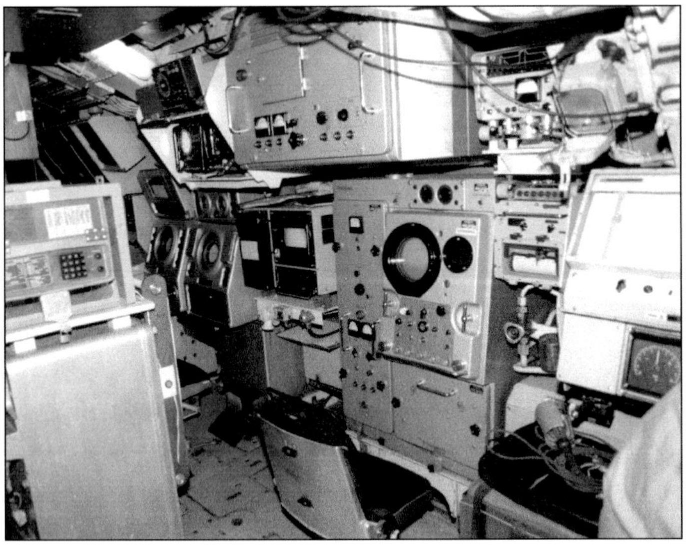

ARA *San Luis'* Control Room. From left to right: Atlas AN-525 A6 passive sonar console; Atlas AN-407 A9 active sonar console and, slightly to its right and above it, the ARUR-10B (ESM) radar warning display and, on the top, the IAG-1 ESM. To the right, the Van der Heem Electronics SPI sound ray path analyser and, in the middle of the photograph the position for the radar operator (Thomson CSF Calypso II) and to its right and above it, the Q-SUA-2 cavitation detector; to the extreme right, the bathythermograph display. Opposite the radar operator position is the Magnavox MX 1102 Satellite Navigator. (via Fernando Azcueta)

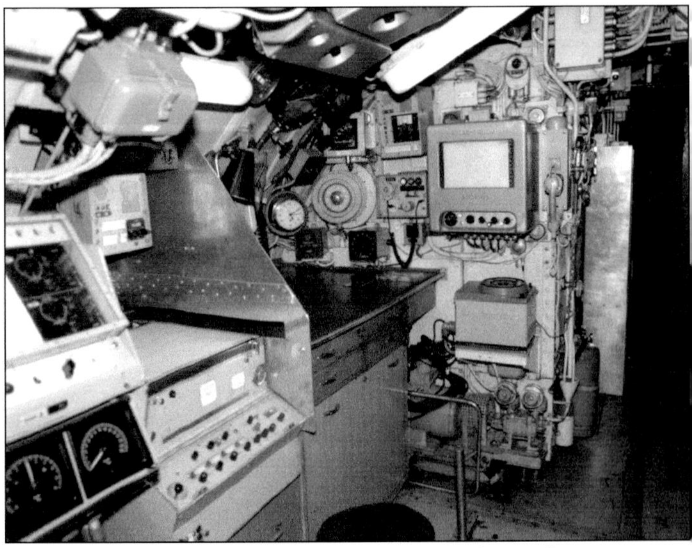

ARA *San Luis'* Control Room. From left to right: bathythermograph display, then the Nedinsco automatic plotting board and the chart table. On the bulkhead, the Krupp Atlas AN681 echo sounder. (via Fernando Azcueta)

ARA *San Luis'* Control Room. From left to right: rudder operator position, bow planes operator position and stern planes operator position. Between the rudder operator position and bow planes operator position is the gyrocompass. (via Fernando Azcueta)

Capitán de Fragata Fernando Azcueta (*San Luis´* Commanding Officer) working on his cabin during the war patrol. (via Fernando Azcueta)

DUUX-2C passive acoustic telemetry sonar. The submarines were also fitted with a Safare-Crouzet DUUG-1D broadband sonar interceptor. This piece of equipment was able to detect any active sonar emissions that made contact with the submarine, and in turn (with the help of the AUUD-1B associated system) indicate the frequency of the intercepted sonar "ping" and the bearing of the vessel making the transmission.

Radar wise, they had a Thomson CSF Calypso II navigation and air-search radar (I-Band) and the ESM suite was also French made (ARUR 10-B and IAG-1 radar interceptors).

They had two Carl-Zeiss periscopes, one for observation (BS-19 model) and the other for attack (AS-18 model). The periscopes came without a stadimeter, which could be used to calculate distances, because it was thought that a modern submariner would only need to use the sonar to arrive at a firing solution.

Finally, the submarines were equipped with a Signaal VM8/24 Fire Control Computer which was used to manage all the information gathered from the various sensors.

During the first few months of 1982 the ARA *Salta* was coming to the end of a period of maintenance at the Mar del Plata Naval Base and, on 2 April, the submarine was in the area of Golfo Nuevo, off Chubut province, in the process of calibrating its DUUX sonar. The crew were completely oblivious of events unfolding on the Falklands/Malvinas islands and news of the landings came, therefore, as a complete surprise for those on board the *Salta*. This included French technicians from Thomson Sintra, who were hurriedly disembarked from the submarine and returned to their country without completing their task.

Even if the *Salta* was, on paper at least, the submarine in best condition in the Argentine submarine fleet, the truth was that it was suffering problems of excessive noise which was coming from somewhere in the propeller shaft. In order to try to resolve this issue, COFUERSUB ordered that the boat go for a comprehensive inspection in a dry-dock. While the *Salta* was undergoing this check-up, at the Puerto Belgrano Naval Base, its *Capitán* was relieved of his command due to health problems.

He was provisionally replaced by a new commander, *Capitán de Fragata* Roberto F. Salinas. Although he had had previously been in command of this submarine in 1979, this sudden change of command did nothing to improve the combat readiness of the vessel.

While in the dry-dock, it was not possible to determine where the problematic noise was emanating from and, in this condition, the submarine carried out some practice torpedo launches on 24 May and 15 June, detailed below, which almost ended in disaster for the submarine and its crew.

As recalled by *Vicealmirante* Juan José Lombardo (Theatre of Operations South Atlantic commander):

Table 2: ARA *Salta*. Torpedo launch exercises

Date	Location	Distance to the target (yards)	Comments
24 May	North of Golfo Nuevo	13,000	The torpedo ran inside the tube for 75 seconds but did not exit it.
24 May	North of Golfo Nuevo	13,000	The torpedo initially ran inside the tube for 54 seconds but did not leave it and then shut down. It reactivated once again 10 hours later, and the motor ran for a further 47 minutes inside the tube.
15 June	North of Golfo Nuevo	11,000	Torpedo successfully swam out the tube. One minute and 41 seconds later the sonar team lost contact with the torpedo. The command wire was then cut by the submarine.
15 June	North of Golfo Nuevo	11,000	Torpedo successfully swam out the tube. The command wire was lost 7,200 yards from the target. It exploded soon after, before hitting the target.

In theory, the *Salta* was the vessel in best condition for combat. It had been in repairs since the beginning of 1982. However, when it went out for trials, a surprisingly intense noise of an indeterminate origin appeared, which rendered the submarine unfit for combat. Its ability to listen had been completely diminished and due to the noise, it would be easily detectable by enemy anti-submarine ships. We made a huge effort to overcome

A view from the sail of submarine *San Luis*, on its way to the war. (via Daniel Mesa)

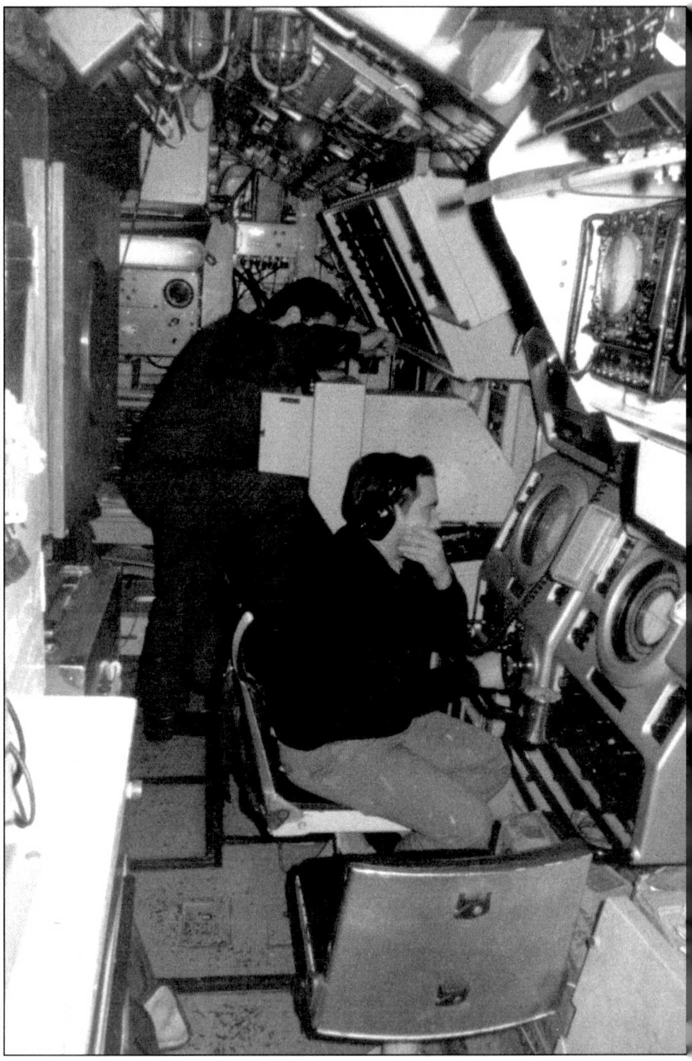

After entering port, two specialists try to repair the broken Signaal VM8/24 Fire Control Computer of ARA *San Luis*. (via Daniel Mesa)

these issues. It went into dry-dock three times. At the end of May it reached a level of noise that, although high, was acceptable. Due to the issues faced by the *San Luis*, I decided to order the *Salta* to sea. I sent it out to carry out two combat torpedo test firings in the Golfo Nuevo while on transit to the Malvinas. It was vital to know what had happened to the weapons that had failed on the *San Luis*. The *Salta* attempted to fire its first torpedo: it activated but remained jammed fast in the torpedo tube. In a brave attempt to get some usable results at whatever cost, a second torpedo launch was attempted, but the torpedo also remained jammed and activated in another torpedo tube. Both weapons were armed and could have exploded at any moment. It was a critical situation and the *Salta* was forced to return to Puerto Belgrano. Despite all the efforts made and having been on the edge of a disaster for both the boat and its crew, the *Salta* wasn't able to take part in the conflict.

Effectively, the submarine was unable to undertake a war patrol. However, the *Salta* was able to exert an influence on the conflict… simply by leaving port.

The *San Luis*

The drums of war on 2 April 1982 came as a bit of a surprise to the commander of the *San Luis* (*Capitán de Fragata* Fernando María Azcueta), which at the time was docked at one of the piers of Mar del Plata Naval Base (BNMP), home base of the small Argentine Navy submarine force. Forty-year-old Azcueta, the son of one of the first submariners of the Argentine Navy was unaware of the Navy High Command decision to assault the Falklands/Malvinas islands, because they wished to keep the operation as secret as possible. Therefore, a decision was taken not to inform the commanders of units not directly involved in Operation Rosario. In fact, the ARA *San Luis* did not receive an order to prepare for a patrol until 24 hours after the assault took place. From that moment, the crew feverishly set to work to make the boat combat capable in the shortest possible time.

The initial condition of the vessel was not entirely satisfactory. It was overdue a visit to a dry-dock and the hull, propeller and refrigeration pipes of the *San Luis* had build-ups of small parasitic crustaceans, which affected its performance and increased its noise level. As there was insufficient time to travel to Puerto Belgrano (Mar del Plata Naval Base lacked a dry-dock), the cleaning process was done in Mar del Plata by divers working 24 hours a day for nearly a week.

Even with hull cleaning carried out, the submarine still had further issues that were not able to be entirely solved before its departure, despite the efforts of the crew and civilian contractors: one of the four diesel engines was non-operational due to a cracked engine block and the other three all had issues which limited their power output; the snorkel regularly allowed sea water into the submarine, a problem which was compounded by a malfunction in the bilge pump and finally, the DUUX system did not give accurate information and was deemed to be non-operational.

Some of the crew of ARA *San Luis* during its war patrol. (via Daniel Mesa)

The training level of the crew had also been affected by the personnel rotation policy of the Argentine Navy: many of the crew were new to the ship and various key posts in the submarine, such those in the fire control systems, were occupied by junior non-commissioned officers. The most experienced submariners in the Argentine Navy were, at the time, in West Germany, supervising the construction of the new TR 1700 boats.

Teniente de Corbeta Luis Seghezzi, was the *San Luis*' incredibly young pilot (Navigation Officer) and had only graduated from the Submarine School in 1981:

> Some had said that we were an inexperienced crew. It was a fact that most of the crew had only spent around three months on board the *San Luis*. Furthermore, for some of us, including myself, that year was our first experience of being part of an operational combat unit. However, this was nothing new for the crews of that class of submarines. A high turnover ensured the largest number of crewmembers were trained in new technologies, bearing in mind that the Argentine Navy was in the midst of incorporating other even more modern units that were currently being built in Germany. That said, had there been a higher level of crew experience in that situation, I don't think it would have guaranteed any better results as nobody in the service had lived an experience like that before.

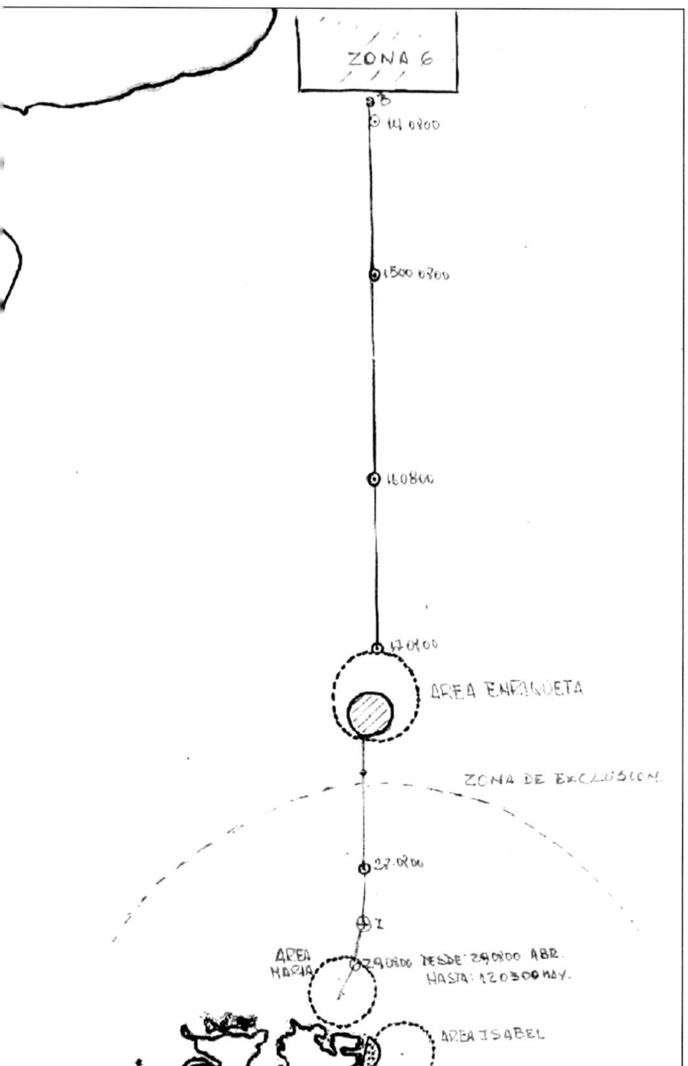

ARA *San Luis*' movements, from its home base to MARIA area. ENRIQUETA was a waiting area outside the Total Exclusion Zone (named on the chart as "Zona de Exclusión"). The submarine went to the surface briefly on 27 April in the afternoon (midway from ENRIQUETA to the Total Exclusion Zone) to investigate a strange noise: it was discovered that a discarded welding torch lay between the casing and the pressure hull! The problem was quickly resolved, and the submarine resumed its voyage south. (ARA *San Luis* War Diary)

Also, while the *San Luis*' command crew were experienced submariners, neither Azcueta nor his second-in-command had any experience in the Type 209s.

Late in the afternoon on 11 April, not a minute later than the scheduled departure time, loaded to the gills with food and water and armed with 10 SST-4 anti-surface wire-guided torpedoes and 14 Mk 37 mod 3 acoustic homing weapons on board, the ARA *San Luis* and its 36 crew members departed Mar del Plata. *Cabo Segundo* Eduardo Lavarello was a marine engineering technician (stoker in Royal Navy´s parlance), crewmember of *San Luis*:

> We set sail on April 11. It was Easter Sunday. We went out at dusk, the weather was not ideal, there was a bit of fog, very ugly cool but, in order to go unnoticed was the right thing, I remember these details since I had to do manoeuvres on deck with the mooring lines. We quickly got lost at night looking for the dive point.
>
> We had to check the displacement, our own noise level and the cooling of the diesel engines. The first two were OK, but the engine cooling system was not at its best. However, the commander and the chief engineer agreed to continue since the area where we had to operate was very cold.

On 17 April 1982 the *San Luis*, following a transit without further problems during which the commander had used the time to further train the crew and deal with some of the remaining mechanical issues, the radio operator received a ciphered message which instructed the

Teniente de Navío Alejandro Alessandrini (ARA *San Luis'* Weapon´s Officer) is ready to investigate a noise. (via Fernando Azcueta)

boat to head to the designated waiting zone, area ENRIQUETA, located to the east of the Golfo San Jorge and close to the Argentine mainland.

At first, as was the case with the British forces, there was a limitation on the use of weapons due to the Rules of Engagement in place. At that time, these could only be used within the Maritime Exclusion Zone and only after a positive identification of the target. The exception to the rule would be if a target was a submerged submarine, which would be presumed to be enemy. These orders were almost identical, initially, to those in place for the British submarines.

Two days later, the VM8/24 Fire Control Computer failed, and its repair was beyond the capabilities of the young crewmembers in charge of its operation. The fire control system is the brain of an attack submarine and it, fed by the diverse sensors searching the outside ocean, allows the submarine to resolve a fire control solution, permitting the firing of either straight-running or homing torpedoes. The VM8/24 underwater fire control system could simultaneously track and prepare fire control solutions for up to three targets, and control three torpedoes aimed at those. The system could be used not only to calculate torpedo lead angles but also to process all sensor data to give target positions and vectors. It could simultaneously display sonar, radar and periscope range, and heading data.

Its inoperability was a devastating blow. It left the submarine without its automatic fire capability and limited it to being able to fire just one torpedo at a time that could be guided by the crew in manual (emergency) mode. As remembered by *Teniente de Navío* Ricardo Alessandrini, *San Luis* Weapon´s Officer:

> The fire control computer was non-operational and left us short of capability in the waiting area. This would limit the number of torpedo firings that could be controlled from the submarine. However, in the submarine service we often practised the old-fashioned method of firing torpedoes by using manual calculations and it was entirely possible to carry out a successful attack with good information about our target.

The Submarine Force Commander (COFUERSUB) acknowledged the problem but decided not to recall the ARA *San Luis* from the waiting area, after evaluating the convenience of having at least one submarine on patrol despite the limitations it was carrying.

Come 26 April, the negotiations over the fate of the islands were practically at a close. COFUERSUB decided to send the *San Luis* to the MARIA patrol area, located to the north of the islands. It arrived there on the 28th.

On the afternoon of the following day, with the military and political situation deteriorating, ARA *San Luis* received the order to destroy any enemy target if located within the Maritime Exclusion Zone around the islands:

> FM COFUERSUB TO SUSL. RESTRICTIONS ON USE OF WEAPONS ANULLED. ANY CONTACT MADE WILL BE ENEMY.

The *Santa Fe*

The ARA *Santa Fe* (S-21) was incorporated into the Argentine Navy in 1971. Prior to this, it had served in the US Navy under the name USS *Catfish*. A Balao-class submarine, it had been delivered in 1944 and served in the Pacific Theatre during the Second World War. In 1948 it was brought up to the Guppy II standard, and a little later it took part in the Korean War. It measured almost 94 metres in length and had a maximum surface speed of 16.4 knots. Its maximum theoretical underwater speed was 14.6 knots.

On paper, the submarine was capable of being continuously submerged for 108 hours, and after this period would need to come to the surface to recharge its batteries or do so via its snorkel. However, the submarine's batteries were almost life-expired and therefore its submerged endurance was significantly reduced.

It could also operate, according to the manuals, up to a depth of 188 metres (616 feet), but the fact was that the old hull of the submarine had difficulty maintaining its depth below periscope depth. Its electronic equipment was obsolete and had its own age-related problems. It had a AN/BQR-2B passive sonar with a maximum range against a snorkelling submarine in ideal conditions about 15-20nm,

A Mk 14 straight running torpedo being loaded aboard an Argentine Guppy-class submarine. (Armada Argentina)

and an AN/BQS-4C active sonar system with a maximum range 6,000 to 8,000 yards, DUUG-1C sonar intercept receiver, SS2 radar and a standard Guppy ESM/ECM suite (AN/BLR-1A, AN/WLR-3A, AN/BLR-6 and AN/BRD-6).

When it came to weapons, it was equipped, when it sailed for its war mission to South Georgia, with 15 Mk 14 straight-run and eight Mk 37 Mod 3 homing torpedoes (the maximum load was 24 torpedoes). The submarine also carried 13 NAE Beacon acoustic noisemakers and 41 FTC (False Target Canister) decoys for protection against homing torpedoes.

Above all else, the *Santa Fe* was a submarine that was months away from being decommissioned which was why the Argentine Navy had not invested too much of its funds in it, nor paid it much attention. It had taken part in Operation Rosario and, following that, returned to its home base of Mar del Plata on 7 April. On arrival, the submarine was suffering from many faults and issues. In the words of its commander, *Capitán de Corbeta* Horacio Alberto Bicain:

> The batteries had a very poor performance; the radio did not function as well as it should; the RATT machine (Radio Automatic Teletype) was non-operational; the bilge pumps only worked at periscope depth and the engines suffered from a notable loss of oil when operating. This was all within the frame of an old and worn-out submarine.

These issues were hastily repaired and although with that done the submarine was still in a precarious condition, it was ready for operations once again on 15 April. A few days prior to this, the submarine and its commander were tasked with a new mission (COFUERSUB 03 "S"/82 order): to transport 20 Marines and their heavy equipment (which included six Bantam anti-tank missiles; a recoilless gun; five 3.5" rocket launchers and communications equipment) to reinforce the detachment at Grytviken in South Georgia, which was still under the control of Argentina at this time. The submarine was to carry out the same role as many Japanese ones did in the last days of the Second World War as transports for isolated garrisons, in islands that could not easily be resupplied by other means due to the naval blockade.

Having delivered and offloaded its passengers and their cargo, their orders were to take up a patrol in the area to the north of South Georgia (Georgias del Sur) and carry out offensive actions against any enemy ships they located. The explanation given for these orders by *Vicealmirante* Lombardo, who had been the commander of the *Santa Fe* ten years previously, was:

> The *Santa Fe* was at the end of its life cycle. According to the schedule drawn up in 1980, the submarine was to be decommissioned in the middle of 1982. It had almost no military value. The journey to South Georgia was a way to give it a task to carry out. It would have been illogical to give this task to a front-line unit which would be more useful to be with the rest of the fleet. We could have used a sea-going tug to do this for us, however, there were not too many of these and they were usually busy with their own work. Besides this, a surface unit did not have any stealth and I felt then, and know it as fact today, that the British were able to track the movement of all our ships at sea. The *Santa Fe* had the possibility to carry out this task without being discovered, which in fact was almost the case. On arrival in the area, if the enemy did not have any specific anti-submarine escorts with them, then the *Santa Fe* would have a degree of tactical advantage over its adversaries.

ARA *San Luis'* torpedo tubes, in the mid-80s. The sign *"cargado"* indicates that the tubes are loaded. (via Fernando Azcueta)

A drill SST-4 torpedo being loaded into submarine ARA *San Luis* in 1981. (Juan Ignacio Rela)

Only in the last hours of the 16 May did the 77 crewmembers (plus the 20 Marines) set off on their mission, leaving their base and heading south.

Argentine Navy submarine launched torpedoes

COFUERSUB had on inventory three models of submarine launched torpedoes: the German made SST-4, the older and US made Mk 37 mod 3 and, finally, the ancient but still capable Mk 14 (also from the US).

The SST-4 (Special Surface Target 4) torpedoes had been delivered to the Argentine Navy in 1974 and 1975 by their manufacturer, AEG-Telefunken. At the time these were one of the most modern submarine

Submarine ARA *San Luis* returning to Mar del Plata Base, from its long endurance patrol. In order to test the capabilities of the then new Type 209 submarines, a patrol in the vicinity of the Falkland/Malvinas islands was ordered by the Argentine Navy High Command in 1975. This was completed satisfactorily and included a night spent on the seabed close to the capital of the islands. (Museo de la Fuerza de Submarinos)

A view from ARA *San Luis'* periscope during an anti-submarine exercise shortly before the war: an Argentine destroyer (probably ARA *Py*) was closing on the submarine. (via Fernando Azcueta)

weapons in the world. The torpedoes, in their export version, had a maximum range of 40,000 yards (36.5 kilometres) at 23 knots and a range of 12,000 yards (11 kilometres) at their maximum speed of 35 knots. When launched, they were connected to the submarine by a copper wire which unreeled from a dispenser inside the torpedo containing 18 kilometres of wire and another dispenser inside the submarine which contained a further nine kilometres. This wire permitted the submarine to guide the torpedo. This SST-4 was a swim-out design – the torpedo swims out of the tube on their own – and could be fired from a submerged submarine at a depth of between four and 100 metres (328 feet).

The weapon, over and above being guided from its parent submarine, was also equipped with its own active/passive sonar in case of either being programmed to carry out an autonomous attack in the terminal phase of its path and near to its target, or could switch to the self-governing mode if the guidance wire was severed for whatever reason. In a text-book attack, the submarine guides the torpedo to the target's vicinity and then it proceeds autonomously to attack it.

According to its manufacturer, the torpedo should be able to acquire a target in passive mode at a distance of 5,000 metres (around 5,500 yards) and in an active mode at a range of 4,000 metres (around 4,400 yards). The Royal Navy also estimated the SST-4's passive detection range against a Leander-class frigate in South Atlantic conditions was 700 metres (around 2,300 feet) versus a ship at 10 knots and 1,400 metres (around 4,600 feet) if the ship's speed was 20 knots.

The export version of the SST-4 did not have a vertical homing capability and could not be ordered to change depth by the submarine once it had been fired. In any case, the torpedo could only attack surface targets. On impacting a target, a contact fuse would be

Impact at last! The former Gearing-class destroyer ARA *Py* sinks after being hit by an SST-4 torpedo launched from Argentine submarine ARA *Santa Cruz* (Type TR 1700), during a live fire exercise on 15 June 1987. It took just five minutes for the ship to disappear under the waves. (Armada Argentina

activated, which would set off a 260 kg (573 lb) warhead. According to the manufacturer, if a torpedo hit the side of a target, it would leave a hole approximately nine metres (30 feet) in diameter. Under these circumstances, a ship would sink in minutes. However, at the time of the start of the conflict this submarine weapon had still not been fully tested by the Argentine Navy.

When these torpedoes first arrived in Argentina, in order to expedite the approval of the torpedo for service, 19 test firings were made (15 by submarine and four from the Lürssen TNC-45 Fast Patrol Boats, which were also equipped with torpedo tubes) of which only eight were totally successful. None of the launches were made with a warhead fitted. However, despite the low level of reliability encountered, the weapon was accepted for service.

In the lapse of time between December 1975 and May 1980 there were no further firings apart from three short distance trial firings in 1977. Then, from May 1980 to March 1982 a further eight firings of SST-4s were carried out with only one of those going to plan: one torpedo was lost and the other six suffered disconnection of the guidance wire during their test runs. Again, none of these tests involved torpedoes with a warhead fitted. Therefore, at the time of the conflict the condition of the torpedoes could not be considered to be optimal.

Why? The manufacturer recommended that the torpedoes be overhauled at least once every ten years and, given they had been manufactured between 1972 and 1973, they were at the limit of their life cycle. However, it was considered that the designed lifespan would only be valid if the torpedoes were stored in controlled conditions of humidity, pressure and temperature. As a suitable torpedo store was not constructed until 1981, the reality was that the torpedoes were already life-expired in 1982.

The gyroscopes fitted to the torpedoes should have been serviced every 48 months. However, the Argentine Navy did not possess any appropriate equipment with which to do this. In 1980, six gyroscopes had been labelled as being non-operational and were sent back to Germany along with a further three for remedial work. Twenty-two remained in Argentina with no guarantee of reliability in use.

The batteries fitted to the torpedoes, manufactured between 1971 to 1972, were thought to have a useful life of between seven and nine years. Between 1979 and 1982, another 13 new batteries had been acquired (making a total of 43 available). COFUERSUB requested, in February 1981, that tests of the batteries be carried out. However, these were never fulfilled and, in April 1982, the *San Luis* embarked some torpedoes with life-expired batteries.

On top of that, there was a design issue with the torpedoes which would render them defective. In order to avoid an international scandal, in September and October 1982, the torpedo manufacturer made an offer to the Argentine Navy, free of charge (as compensation), to supply a quantity of spares as well as the servicing and repair of the existing weapons. In 1984, and despite the arms embargo Argentina was under, a large part of a torpedo was shipped to West Germany so that studies of them could be carried out and the results sent back to Argentina.

However, the subject of torpedoes does not finish there. On the 17 June, a few days after the end of hostilities on the islands, technician Eduardo Lopez and engineer Raul Pereira were working on the *San Luis* at the Puerto Belgrano Naval Base. Lopez, who was a civilian contractor working for the navy, discovered that a switchboard, which supplied the electrical feed for the torpedo's gyroscopes, had had the polarity reversed. This inversion meant that the any torpedo would lose its bearing once fired. Sadly, as Lopez left the submarine, he suffered an unfortunate accident. As he was leaving the submarine through the external door, which was undergoing maintenance and was disconnected, it fell back on him, killing him instantly. However, he had already passed the information regarding his discovery to Pereira.

It was never determined whether this had been a case of sabotage, if the submarine simply went to war unaware of this issue or if this was a product of the repairs that had been carried out on it. However, the opinion of the submariners on board the *San Luis* was clear. According to *Teniente de Navío* Alessandrini, *San Luis*' Weapon´s Officer:

> It was impossible that the vessel had left for war with this issue (the inversion of the wires). When the submarines were due to leave port, they would prepare the torpedoes and carry out pre-departure simulated firings with each of the torpedoes. If there had been a

Table 3: Argentine Navy submarine launched torpedoes					
Weapon	**Guidance System**	**Target**	**Warhead Weight (lb)**	**Operational range (yards)**	**Submarine**
SST-4	Wire-guided. Passive and active sonar capabilities	Anti-ship	573	12,000 at 35 knots / 40,000 at 23 knots	ARA *San Luis* / ARA *Salta*
Mk 37 mod 3	Gyroscope (initial), passive (cruise) and active sonar (terminal)	Anti-ship / Anti-submarine	330	10,000 at 26 knots / 23,000 at 17 knots	ARA *San Luis* / ARA *Salta* / ARA *Santa Fe*
Mk 14	Gyroscope	Anti-ship	643	4,500 at 46 knots / 9,000 at 31.1 knots	ARA *Santa Fe*

change in polarity of the wires, this fact would have come to light prior to departure. It was impossible.

What is fact, however, is that the SST-4 torpedoes fired during the conflict did not appear to function correctly. We will see it in detail later.

The Mk 37 homing torpedo had been introduced in 1956, mainly as an answer to the increasing threat of the submarines of the Soviet Union. It had an effective firing range of 23,000 yards (21 kilometres) at 17 knots or 10,000 yards (9.15 kilometres) at 26 knots. With the introduction of newer, better performing submarines, from 1967 the Mk 37 underwent a series of improvements which increased the range of the sonar (from 700 to 1,000 yards) and the ability to attack targets at a greater depth. However, its Achilles heel of its relatively low running speed of only 26 knots remained.

From 1972 the weapon began to be replaced in the US Navy by the newer Mk 48. Nevertheless, the Mod 3 version that the Argentine Navy possessed were also still used by several other navies. Even so, by 1982, due to their age and maintenance requirements (after all, these were weapons that still used vacuum tubes) presented the submarine crews with continual issues. According to a submarine officer of the Argentine Navy: "I never saw a Mk 37 working correctly. I took part in numerous test launches from Salta class submarines. Something always failed..."

The Mk 14 was a straight-run torpedo which had been designed in 1931, had overcome serious problems experienced by its initial versions and had become the standard submarine weapon of the US Navy during the Second World War. At the end of that conflict a large stock of these torpedoes remained, many of them being transferred in quantity to friendly nations' navies. The Argentine Navy had a lot of experience in the use of these weapons which were simple and easy to maintain.

The Mk 14 had a steam turbine with a compressed air tank and had a maximum range of 9,000 yards (8.2 kilometres). The torpedo would be fired in a salvo to ensure the maximum chance to hit a target and the results obtained would not have been too different to those achieved by the British with their Mk 8 torpedoes which were used to sink both the ARA *General Belgrano* and, after the war, the burned hulk of the RFA *Sir Galahad*.

4
BRITISH ANTI-SUBMARINE FORCES AND THEIR TACTICS IN THE SOUTH ATLANTIC

The Royal Navy helicopters, ships and equipment and how they operated

The Royal Navy's main ASW (anti-submarine warfare) aerial platform during the conflict was the Westland Sea King HAS.5 (HAS for Helicopter Anti Submarine). This new ASW version of the helicopter, at the time of the conflict, had only been in service for less than a year. These machines were split between two units: 820 NAS (Naval Air Squadron) under the command of Lt Cdr R.J.S. Wykes-Sneyd, with its 11 helicopters based on HMS *Invincible* and 826 NAS, commanded by Lt Cdr D.J.S. Squier, with its nine helicopters and based on HMS *Hermes*.

In addition to the HAS.5s, A Flight of 824 NAS, under the command of Lt Cdr I.S. McKenzie operated its two older ASW versions of the Sea King (the HAS.2), from the support ship RFA *Olmeda*. Three further HAS.2s of C Flight 824 NAS were based on RFA *Fort Grange*. They arrived in the area at the beginning of June and had only a minor ASW role.

The Westland WS-61 Sea King was the British built version of the popular Sikorsky S-61. The main difference between this and the US version of the aircraft was that it was fitted with two Rolls-Royce Gnome turbines as well as the flight control and electronic systems being of UK origin. The new HAS.5 model was fitted with a new radar, a MEL Super Searcher, with a greater range; modern ESM equipment and a new AQS-902 acoustic processing system.

It was a medium sized helicopter with a maximum loaded weight of 21,000 lbs, a range of 664 nautical miles and a top speed of 129 mph. The usual crew of the "Cab" was made up of four servicemen: Pilot (P1), Co-pilot (P2), Observer (FLOBS) and Aircrewman. Unlike other services, the Observer was qualified as a tactical coordinator and was responsible, among other things, for operating communications and making the navigation and weapon employment decisions.

The main sensor on the aircraft was the GEC-Plessey Type 195M dipping sonar. This sonar had both an active and passive mode with a frequency of some 10 kHz and could be used up to a depth of 246 metres (807 feet): the sonar transducer (also called sonar body) was lowered from a helicopter in a stationary hover over the surface of the sea to a depth required by the operator inside the helicopter. The

Westland Sea King HAS.5 ZA135 of 810 Naval Air Squadron, visiting Koksijde Air Base. (Belgium) on 19 July 1986. (Chris England)

sonar was not easy to maintain and gave problems to its end users. Lieutenant Steve George, from 820 NAS:

> The dunking sonar was a real challenge – it required constant work to keep going, and the workload on the radio trade and the associated sonar workshops was, at times, really huge. The other radio item that was really poor was our main UHF radio – the ancient ARC/52. These failed for a habit. In the end, we developed ways of changing sonar and radio components (or whole boxes, or groups of boxes) while the aircraft were turning and burning on the deck.

It was principally used in the active mode during the conflict as it was considered that the small and stealthy Argentine Type 209 submarines (the *San Luis* and *Salta*), in the words of the commander of 820 NAS: "were not considered to be valid targets for passive operations, except during their short and infrequent snorting cycle."

In addition to this, intelligence reports prior to the start of hostilities opined that given the lack of sea depth, scarce oceanographic and conductivity information for the area around the islands it was not recommended to use the sonar in the passive mode. The passive mode (NATO's main method of detecting Soviet submarines in the 80s), it is worth clarifying, meant that the sonar would pick up the sounds emitted by external sources on or under the surface of the sea. The active mode was where sound waves were emitted by the equipment into the water and would pick up any echoes from objects in its path, in a similar way to how a radar works in air warfare. The problem with active sonar is that the sound waves emitted can be detected by anyone who is listening, and at a range greater than their own detection range. For this reason, its use was usually avoided if possible.

Sonar is the most important piece of equipment in anti-submarine warfare for the simple reason that sound is the ideal way to detect a submerged object. Both light and radio waves, except for extremely low frequency which was used for communicating with submerged submarines, only penetrate a few metres into the sea, which meant that their ability to detect a submarine was very limited.

Sonars came in various forms. The sonar transducer of the Type 195M or the underwater arrays of the SOSUS system are only two examples. They are also to be found mounted in the hulls of ships and submarines or towed by the same. The other type comes in the form of a buoy deployed by either an aircraft, helicopter or ship and is known as a sonobuoy.

The sonar operator's job was to interpret the information gathered by the device. With older equipment, such as those used in the Second World War, the operator only had his ears with which to try to decipher the information received. In the case of more modern equipment, he was aided by computer, which also provided visual references.

Sound does not move through water in the same way it moves through the atmosphere. Variations in temperature and salinity, maritime fauna (and other countless factors) affect the way that the sound waves move through water. The existence of a thermal layer in the sea should also be considered. At the time of year that the conflict took place, this would be found in the Area of Operations, except in the very shallow shelf waters, at around 200 to 300 feet (approximately 61 to 91 metres). This layer causes an abrupt change in the sea conditions and sound can only partially penetrate it. This makes it ideal for submarines wishing to escape detection to move under what is called the thermocline. Also, it can be difficult for a submarine to detect another submarine (or ship) on the other side of the layer.

Other equipment, such as Magnetic Anomaly Detector (MAD) only had a secondary use in submarine detection. A MAD detects small variations in the Earth's magnetic field based on the fact that a mass of a ferrous material would alter this field, and therefore be detectable. However, the equipment's range was very small and therefore its use as a tool to search for submarines was limited.

It was principally used to help establish a contact classification of an already detected contact or as a method to directly establish the attack criteria on a contact. The magnetic sensor was in a towed device (called the "MAD bird" in US Navy and Royal Navy parlance), in order to reduce the magnetic effects of the helicopter itself. Aircraft like the Nimrod had a MAD boom on the tail.

Four of 826 NAS's Sea Kings had been recently fitted with MADs, although they were not considered to be too reliable (specially over

A Sea King HAS.2 of 824 NAS C Flight on the aft deck of RFA *Fort Grange* (A385) during the 1982 conflict. (John Osmond)

Sea King HAS.5 ZA131 with its Type 195 sonar transducer hanging beneath. RNAS Yeovilton Air Show, 1984. ZA131 deployed down south with 826 NAS, based on HMS *Hermes*. (Nick Weight)

shallow waters) and a further four Lynx helicopters were fitted with them. During the war the United States authorised the delivery of fifteen far more capable AN/ASQ–81 (V) MAD sets to the United Kingdom for use in their ASW Sea Kings, but these systems were not deployed in the South Atlantic.

The final piece in the Sea Kings' detection kit were the LOFAR (passive) and active sonobuoys. There were installed only in the Sea King HAS.5 (along with the Lightweight Acoustic Processing and Display System – LAPADS), but its use in the Falklands/Malvinas conflict was very limited.

The final aerial ASW specialist machines of the fleet came in the form of two rather elderly Westland Wessex HAS.3s of 737 NAS. These machines remained in Royal Navy service to provide an anti-submarine capability for the remaining, and obsolete by 1982, County Class destroyers, two of which were in the Task Force.

The Wessex HAS.3 was a medium-size helicopter (maximum loaded weight of 13,500lbs, range of 270 nautical miles and top speed of 132 mph), with a usual crew of four. Its electronic suite and avionics were like those of the Sea King HAS.2 and it was equipped with the Type 195M dunking sonar and ARI 5955 radar. One Wessex, XP142 nicknamed "Humphrey", was based on HMS *Antrim* and the other, XM837 nicknamed "Willie", was based on HMS *Glamorgan*. Humphrey would go on to have quite an eventful war, as will be seen later in the book. Willie, however, was somewhat less fortunate and would not survive the war, being destroyed by the land based Exocet missile that hit *Glamorgan* on the morning of 12 June.

In addition to these Sea Kings and the pair of Wessex, the British Fleet had a large number of other Westland types at its disposal. There was a total of 19 Lynx HAS.2 helicopters (815 NAS), 10 Wasp HAS.1 (829 NAS) and 48 Wessex HU.5 (847 and 848 NAS) spread amongst the various ships of the Task Force.

Some, those based on the frigates and destroyers, were equipped with anti-submarine gear and the capability to drop torpedoes or depth charges (overall, 29 helicopters had weapon delivery systems but no sonar installed). However, this would be very much used in a secondary role:

> None of the Lynx, Wasp or Wessex HU.5 had any real ASW location capability although some of the Lynx did have a MAD fitted. Whilst at sea, the Wessex were primarily used for stores and passenger transfer – they were needed ashore once the soldiers got there. The Wasps had a reactive ASW capability as they could carry homing torpedoes and were probably on alert for this some of the time. The Lynx also had an ASW anti-torpedo capability and a few were used occasionally in this role but were primarily tasked with anti-surface either on searches or carrying Sea Skua missiles. Another important role for the Lynx, as strange as it may sound, was Airborne Early Warning. They had the Orange Crop ESM equipment to listen to enemy radar and these were used to warn of any Etendard attacks. They also did their share of load lifting and also spotting the fall of shot for the ships bombarding the shore. (Lieutenant Larry Jeram-Croft, 815 NAS, HMS *Andromeda*)

It is also worth mentioning the Sea King HC.4 Commandos that were also deployed with the fleet (845 and 846 Naval Air Squadrons).

Submarine ARA *San Luis* with its masts up. (via Daniel Mesa)

A pre-war shot of a Sea King HAS.5 streaming its MAD bird. (Royal Navy)

County class destroyer HMS *Antrim* (D18) during the Falklands/Malvinas War. Humphrey (its Wessex HAS.3) is also clearly visible in this photograph. (MoD)

These helicopters had no ASW role and were used mainly for transport duties, alongside the Wessex HU.5s.

Finally, anti-submarine Sea Kings HAS.2 of the hastily formed 825 NAS broke the invisible barrier between "Pingers" and "Junglies" (the anti-submarine helicopters were informally known in the Royal Navy as "Pingers" while the Commando helicopters were known as "Junglies"), using the helicopters (striped of its ASW equipment) in the troop transport/cargo role.

Given the nature of the conflict, the helicopters carried out the main role in the anti-submarine war as the warships also had to deal with the problem of the Argentine air threat, which was both greater and more flexible. However, in reality, all the ships of the Task Force would have some kind of anti-submarine role to play.

The Royal Navy's specialist anti-submarine warship in 1982 was the recently introduced and modern Type 22 frigate. This class was represented by HMS *Brilliant* and HMS *Broadsword* in the Task Force. However, all the British warships were equipped with modern sonars and had a great deal of training in the war against submarines. Even ships such as the Type 42 destroyers, which were specialised in the anti-air role, also possessed a credible ASW capability and gear.

Of the 22 warships in the theatre, from 12 April to 14 June, 17 were equipped with the Type 184M sonar, two with the Type 177 and three with the Type 2016 sonar (whilst all also had the Type 162). All of these sonar types were hull mounted.

The most modern of the sonars mentioned was the Type 2016 manufactured by Plessey (Ferranti being responsible for the powerful 64k memory FM1600B computer utilized for signal processing). It was a medium frequency computerised sonar and the prototype of which had been fitted to HMS *Broadsword* in 1978. The sonar had the capability to use two separate transmitters operating on the 5.5, 6.5 and 7.5 kHz frequency in order to minimize inter-ship interference. It could automatically detect and track submerged targets. It functioned reliably during the conflict and the only time one of the systems failed was when one of the ships housing the sonar suffered 30mm cannon damage from an attacking Argentine aircraft. Nevertheless, it did have its limitations and was criticized for its lack of direct (sound) output. According to the CO of HMS *Broadsword* (Captain W.R. Canning):

It could not guarantee discrimination between a submarine and some forms of marine life. This has always been a sonar problem, but without an audio facility, assessments had to be based on computer information and operator experience. It was found that whales and shoals of fish regularly gave a high weight of evidence and a submarine-like image. During CASEXES, HMS *Courageous* would have been classified marine life by an experienced operator, based on computer suggestion. It is considered that an audio facility should be provided at the surveillance display to aid assessments still further…It rejected bottom contacts out of hand as non-subs. This was potentially embarrassing in an area where the enemy was known to be capable of bottoming.

A Lynx from HMS *Arrow* (F13) releasing a drill Mk 44 torpedo in the Mediterranean Sea, in 1979. This particular torpedo failed to inflate its recovery collar and was lost. (John Osmond)

Westland Wasp HAS.1 XS543 in Middle Wallop on 25 July 1982. The helicopter was armed with AS.12 missiles. Shortly after the photograph was taken, it was sold to the Royal New Zealand Navy and it is now in the Air Force Museum of New Zealand. (Chris England)

The Graseby Type 184M was the most common sonar in the Task Force. It operated at 6, 7.5 and 9 kHz and could automatically track multiple targets. It relied to a large extent on target movement for detection or classification. The Type 184 was designed as a successor of the older Type 177 set and introduced all-around scanning and simultaneous active and passive (for torpedo detection) operation. The sonar was able to detect a 45-knot steam torpedo at 6,000 yards whilst the owning ship was moving at the considerable speed of 18 knots. Even though a modern set, it was considered to be both unreliable and difficult to maintain. Also, in the words of the commander of HMS *Glasgow*: "it is most unlikely that sonar 184 had any real capability for detecting submarines of the size of the 209 class. The abysmal performance of this set is of the greatest concern…recommend sonar 184 be replaced by an improved sonar."

The Kelvin-Hughes Type 162 sonar, for its part, was used for the detection of bottomed submarines (submarines that positioned themselves on the seabed). This sonar operated at 50 kHz and had a scale of 300, 600 and 1,200 yards, the latter only in the M version. It was an old design, which had entered service in 1948 (and in 1951 detected the wreck of submarine *Affray*). Despite its age, it was reliabl and did not receive much criticism for its performance in the conflict

Finally, the Type 177 was an aged set, fitted to the two Rothesa class frigates in the Task Force (HMS *Plymouth* and HMS *Yarmouth* the oldest frigates in the fleet). This was also a relatively old design accepted for service in 1957, that operated, like Type 184, in the 6 7.5 or 9 kHz band. It had a limited performance for the time. In goo conditions, with sea state 1 or 2 and without a thermal layer, the se could detect a submarine at a range of 18,000 yards. The detectio

HMS *Broadsword* (F88) in a 1982 exercise with the US Navy. (US Navy)

range diminished somewhat in sea-state 2-3 and with a thermal layer to 8,000 yards and in the worst scenario, with a sea-state 4 or 5 and a surface layer, the expected range was only 3,000 yards. Also, Type 177 used a flat transducer to scan a sector. Sector operation was acceptable when the sonar was designed, because submarines would be limited to 15 knots, but with modern submarines operating at higher speeds, the sonar lost the contacts, specially at close range (Type 177 searched too slowly and over a very narrow sector of only 40-degrees).

None of these sonar types, despite their issues and in some cases their age, stopped being of use. It is also worth considering that the 177, 184 and 2016 sonar made a lot of detections of whales in active mode, which were much smaller than the submarines of the Argentine Navy.

Besides sonar, it was also observed that an Argentine submarine could be located when it communicated with its base. Therefore, it was recommended that close attention be paid to the radio systems on board the warships as well as their ESM (Electronic Support Measures) equipment. Finally, it was known that the Argentine submarines would be required to snorkel every now and again. Therefore, radar would continue to be a relevant tool in the ASW tool kit.

The Royal Air Force's role in anti-submarine protection

The Royal Air Force (RAF) had, within the United Kingdom defence organization, a very important role in anti-submarine warfare. Until just a few years ago, this role was carried out by its Hawker Siddeley Nimrod maritime patrol aircraft (MPA), now retired. This aircraft was a modification of the de Havilland Comet airliner and would carry a crew trained in all kinds of over water missions.

During the conflict, from 6 April, there were always between two and five Nimrod aircraft at RAF Wideawake, the name of the airbase on Ascension Island. The first Nimrods to arrive at Ascension were the MR1s operated by 42 Squadron RAF. These were soon replaced (from 18 April) by MR2s (120, 201 and 206 squadrons).

At the start of May, some of the MR2s were converted to MR2P standard. The main modification to get the aircraft to this standard was the installation of an in-flight refuelling probe, something that exponentially increased its operating range.

The Nimrod MR2s were fitted, in terms of anti-submarine equipment, with a modern EMI Searchwater radar, which replaced the obsolete ASV21 radar of the previous model, Marconi AQS-901 acoustic processors for sonobuoys and a Loral 1017 Yellow Gate Electronic Support Measures (ESM) system. The MR2s had only recently been introduced to service and, from 26 February to 29 March 1982, a few aircraft from 206 squadron had been deployed to Homestead AFB, a United States Air Force base near Miami, in order to be assessed at the US Navy's Atlantic Undersea Test and Evaluation Center (AUTEC). While the MR2's sensors were being evaluated, two other Nimrod MR2s (XV230 and XV253) were also in the United States, this time in Albuquerque (New Mexico), carrying out weapon tests at the Naval Weapons Evaluation Facility (NWEF). Everything worked as expected and they returned to their base in Kinloss in Scotland on 3 March.

The kipper fleet was at top performance for its forthcoming anti-submarine war in the South Atlantic.

In the words of RAF Air Marshal Sir John Bagot Curtiss:

> the submarine threat was small but significant, but the principal threat to the transiting Task Group and following units, many of them unarmed STUFT, was identified as coming from Argentine naval surface forces, especially the *25 de Mayo* (the Argentine aircraft carrier).

Therefore, the principal mission for the Nimrod fleet was to aid in the protection of Ascension Island, carry out medium and long range reconnaissance flights as well as maintaining open lines of maritime communication between the fleet and the island without getting directly involved in ASW support of the former.

The classic tactic to harass a conventional diesel/electric submarine, from the air, was to maintain continuously an aircraft in its area of operations for 24 hours, forcing it to the surface or at least to snorkel, which would substantially increase the possibilities of it being detected, and therefore attacked and destroyed.

This was the tactic employed in 1962 during the Cuban missile crisis against the Soviet Foxtrot class submarines. For this tactic to be successful two conditions are necessary: first, there is good initial intelligence about the area of operations of the submarine and second that there is a capability to maintain continuous operations.

However, even if the initial intelligence about the Argentine submarines was not generally too bad, what was true was that the Nimrods were unable to operate close to the Falkland/Malvinas islands for very long. Even with a huge air to air refuelling effort, the

Table 4: Royal Navy escorts

Ship	Captain	Type	Class	Commissioned	Anti-submarine weapons	Helicopter carried	Date entering Falklands grid	Damage suffered
HMS *Bristol*	A. Grose	Destroyer	Type 82	1973	IKARA single launcher / Limbo 3-barrelled DC mortar		23 May	
HMS *Antrim*	B.G. Young	Destroyer	County	1970		1 x Wessex	17 April	Major damage
HMS *Glamorgan*	M.E. Barrow	Destroyer	County	1966	2 × triple STWS tubes	1 x Wessex	24 April	Major damage
HMS *Cardiff*	M.G.T. Harris	Destroyer	Type 42	1979	2 × triple STWS tubes	1 x Lynx	23 May	
HMS *Coventry*	D. Hart-Dyke	Destroyer	Type 42	1978	2 × triple STWS tubes	1 x Lynx	20 April	Sunk
HMS *Exeter*	H.M. Balfour	Destroyer	Type 42	1980	2 × triple STWS tubes	1 x Lynx	19 May	
HMS *Glasgow*	A.P. Hoddinott	Destroyer	Type 42	1979	2 × triple STWS tubes	1 x Lynx	20 April	Moderate damage
HMS *Sheffield*	S. Salt	Destroyer	Type 42	1975		1 x Lynx	20 April	Sunk
HMS *Brilliant*	J.F. Coward	Frigate	Type 22	1981	2 × triple STWS2 tubes	2 x Lynx	20 April	Minor damage
HMS *Broadsword*	W.R. Canning	Frigate	Type 22	1979	2 × triple STWS tubes	2 x Lynx	25 April	Moderate damage
HMS *Active*	Cdr P.C.B. Canter	Frigate	Type 21	1977		1 x Wasp	23 May	
HMS *Alacrity*	Cdr C.J.S. Craig	Frigate	Type 21	1977		1 x Lynx	25 April	
HMS *Ambuscade*	Cdr P.J. Mosse	Frigate	Type 21	1975	2 × triple STWS tubes	1 x Lynx	18 May	
HMS *Antelope*	Cdr N. Tobin	Frigate	Type 21	1975	2 × triple STWS tubes	1 x Lynx	18 May	Sunk
HMS *Ardent*	Cdr A. West	Frigate	Type 21	1977		1 x Lynx	13 May	Sunk
HMS *Arrow*	Cdr P.J. Bootherstone	Frigate	Type 21	1975		1 x Lynx	20 April	Minor damage
HMS *Avenger*	H.M. White	Frigate	Type 21	1978	2 × triple STWS tubes	1 x Lynx	23 May	
HMS *Argonaut*	C.H. Layman	Frigate	(Type 12I) Leander 2B	1967	2 × triple STWS tubes	1 x Lynx	13 May	Major damage
HMS *Penelope*	Cdr P.V. Rickard	Frigate	(Type 12I) Leander 2B	1963	2 × triple STWS tubes	1 x Lynx	23 May	
HMS *Minerva*	Cdr S.H.G .Johnston	Frigate	(Type 12I) Leander 2A	1966	2 × triple STWS tubes	1 x Lynx	23 May	
HMS *Yarmouth*	Cdr A. Morton	Frigate	Type 12M (Rothesay)	1960	Limbo 3-barrelled DC mortar	1 x Wasp	25 April	
HMS *Plymouth*	D.Pentreath	Frigate	Type 12M (Rothesay)	1961	Limbo 3-barrelled DC mortar	1 x Wasp	17 April	Major damage

time on task could not exceed three hours. According to a then young member of 206 squadron deployed to Ascension:

> The main task was anti-surface warfare. There was no planned ASW activity, for the simple reason that there was little or no intelligence (that we were briefed on) about the Argentine submarines, and the Nimrod had a very tight fuel plan at that distance from Ascension. Effective ASW operations would have required solid intelligence about the sub's positions, and the ability to detect, track and prosecute (and obtain attack clearance from Northwood) within a very short timescale. It just wasn't feasible at that range.
>
> But our Tac Nav said we were dropping random Jezebel buoys as we moved east to west on our ASuW search tracks, and he stated if there had been a sniff of a contact on a buoy, he would have

HMS *Yarmouth* (F101) pictured from the flight deck of HMS *Cardiff* (D108) with HMS *Andromeda* following behind. June 1982. (Ken Griffiths)

A Sea King helicopter "in the dip": hovering while lowering the transducer into the water. This photograph was taken during NATO Exercise NORTHERN WEDDING 86. (US Navy)

Hawker Siddeley Nimrod MR1 XV244 at RAF St Mawgan on 14 April 1981. On 5 April 1982 two 42 Sqn Nimrod MR1 aircraft, XV244 and XV258 departed to Ascension Island to form the first permanent RAF detachment as part of Operation Corporate. XV244 returned to St Mawgan on 18 April. (Chris England)

> attacked it immediately as he assumed there were no friendlies in the area! Could have been very messy if the submarine situation (ARG/UK and Soviet) was more complicated than we thought! However, Tac Nav stated that with the ROE we were operating under, he would have had no hesitation in attacking any submarine contact.

The anti-submarine role of the Nimrod fleet was, thus, limited.

The aircraft carried out two types of search missions, surface search missions with a secondary anti-submarine role, first whilst unarmed and then armed from 20 April. The first type of mission was carried out up to a radius of 400 nautical miles from Ascension Island and which was carried out one or two times per day. During these flights, the position of the Soviet spy ship, the *Zaporozhye,* which had trailed the British Task Force south, would be updated and its crew reminded that they were not being left alone.

Possibly the most important anti-submarine task carried out close to Ascension took place on the 18 April. A Nimrod was called to help with the classification of a possible submarine. However, the submarine turned out to be a whale which had given the Task Force rather a shock. The incident started at 0920 when the Chief Engineering Officer on board the support ship RFA *Olmeda* reported having sighted a periscope. At 0957, the contact was located by frigates HMS *Alacrity* and HMS *Broadsword* (the latter also reported a detection of an "Argentine submarine radar"), which were joined soon afterwards by Sea King HAS.2 helicopters from A flight 824 NAS based on *Olmeda*. At 1030, they were joined by a Nimrod which wasted no time in classifying the contact as NONSUB, having sighted a group of whales.

A Victor tanker refuelling a Nimrod MR2 during a long-range sortie over the South Atlantic in 1982. (MoD)

As the CO of HMS *Alacrity* later wrote:

> During the transit south and our early days in the Total Exclusion Zone, there were several incidents of jittery overreactions (often against substantial marine life or unusually deep pockets of temperature/salinity variation). Most notably, a 12-hour series of over-reactive "sub-chasing" took place just as the Task Group sailed from Ascension; this was triggered by a "periscope" sighting from RFA *Olmeda*. It transpired that our confident sonar contacts came from resident shoals of substantial marine life (later described as a "whale of overreaction"!). Thankfully we were refused the use of our sub-surface weapons due to the unconvincing classification of these contacts, else we would have wasted much ordnance. But over all this time, we were at least gathering familiarity with alien waters and the prospect of facing a capable and motivated foe better equipped for this fighting environment. Complacent – we were not!

The second mission type was the long-range surface search which was carried out up to 1,900 nautical miles from Ascension and required the support of air-to-air tanker aircraft. These sorties were more sporadic and provided important intelligence about the movements of Argentine naval units, or indeed the absence of them. The principal sensor during these missions was the EMI Searchwater radar as well as electronic surveillance and communication monitoring of the Argentine forces. The crews were also made aware of the probable areas of operation of the Argentine boats and were tasked with searching for them with sonobuoys, even though the chances of locating enemy submarines was low due to the lack of precise information about their location and the time available for searching.

Derek Straw was aboard one of the MR2s on the 18 May, during a sortie which required in-flight refuelling and came as close as 60 miles from the Argentine coast. He recalled that it got close to the coast to the north of Río Gallegos:

> Soon we were in the probability area for the Argentinian submarine where we dropped Jezebel sonobuoys as we went and monitored them for as long as RF range was held. It was a long shot for detection against an ultra-quiet conventional submarine, but there was an outside chance if it was returning to home base it might be snorting. There were no suspicious contacts and we did not have a great deal of time to loiter should we have gained contact. Any confirmed submarine contact classified non-UK would have seen us attack the buoy it was held on; a target that quiet had to be very close to the buoy, so our torpedoes would have stood a chance of acquisition.

Hawker Siddeley Nimrod MR2P (XV233) at Fairford, July 1991. (Chris England)

A Valiant class submarine (either HMS *Valiant* or HMS *Warspite*) in 1986. (US Navy)

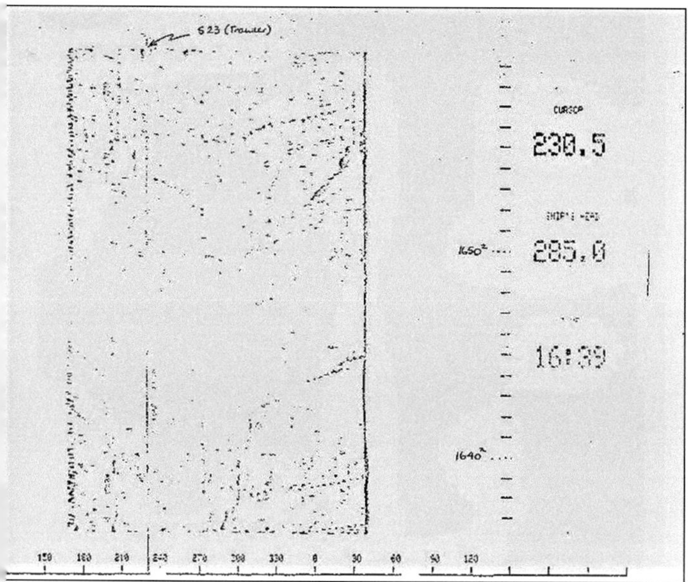

HMS *Valiant*'s passive sonar display print, 17 May 1982. ARA *San Luis* was near there, but it was not detected by the British SSN. (HMS *Valiant* Report of Proceedings)

The Nimrod generally flew both type of missions from 20 April with three Mk 46 torpedoes and four 1,000 lb bombs in its internal weapons bay. During the conflict, five Nimrods were modified to be able to carry the modern and recently produced Sting Ray anti-submarine torpedo: ten of these weapons arrived, by air, at Ascension on 23 April and were carried in no time.

Submarine vs Submarine

In British naval strategy, the hunter-killer submarine held an important role in anti-submarine duties. Missions to locate and follow Soviet submarines were very common (the *Superb*'s task on late March 1982 was a clear example), both against attack and missile boats – the latter being full of strategic nuclear missiles. However, the underwater antagonists of the time were mostly large and noisy and were generally easy to locate thanks to good initial intelligence provided by the SOSUS system. In the South Atlantic, the situation was different.

The British submarines involved in the conflict were part of Task Force 324, isolated from the surface fleet, and commanded by the Flag Officer Submarines, Vice-Admiral Sir Peter Herbert, from the Northwood naval headquarters.

During the conflict with Argentina, five nuclear-powered attack submarines: HMS *Conqueror*, HMS *Splendid*, HMS *Spartan*, HMS *Valiant* and HMS *Courageous* along with a single conventional submarine (HMS *Onyx*), were sent to the South Atlantic. But only *Conqueror*, *Valiant* and *Courageous* were deployed with a clip-on Type 2024 towed array sonar (a system of hydrophones towed behind the submarine on a cable, in order to keep the sensor away from the submarine's own noise), a device especially useful to detect enemy submarines.

Different to their usual NATO role, as described above, the submarines were not given an anti-submarine role as their primary task. It was considered to be too challenging given the inherent problems of detecting a silent Type 209 submarine and the complete lack of knowledge about it amongst the Royal Navy's sonar operators. As disclosed in a post-war report:

> Our in-service passive submarine sonar, both hull-mounted and towed array are optimized against Soviet nuclear submarines, and insufficient attention is given to diesel-powered submarines, hence the use of narrowband systems which might have given some area search capability, particularly during enemy snort cycles, was inhibited by lack of knowledge on distinctive threat frequencies and the absence of a wide-band analyser.

It was assessed the Argentine Type 209s had a sonar advantage of about 3dB (Sonar -5dB, platform +8dB) over a British nuclear submarine, so there was even a chance that the hunter becomes the hunted! Nevertheless, the mission to sink the *San Luis* was assigned to Task Force 324 units on two occasions. These occurred when it was determined, thanks to communications intelligence, that the submarine would be travelling to a particular area and there was an opportunity to intercept it during transit.

The closest that the Royal Navy Submarine Service came to sinking the Argentine boat came when HMS *Valiant* received the order to attack the *San Luis* as it made its way back to its home base. However, although the initial intelligence they possessed was accurate, and having used both active and passive sonar, the crew of the submarine were unable to locate its prey.

At 1030 on 17 May, HMS *Valiant* was in the location where the Argentine submarine was expected to pass. The submarine sonar team predicted detection range of the sonar against a Type 209 submarine was of not more than 2,000 yards on its main motors and 10,000 yards while snorkelling. However, it was not expected to be doing the latter so close to its base.

The plan they came up with was to wait for it and carry out a surprise attack. Notwithstanding, not long after arriving at the location where they were going to wait, they detected, both by sonar and visually, a trawler which confused their towed array picture with "bursts of cavitation, flutter, diesel signature and tonals". On top of this there was a great deal of marine-life activity. With such a confusing panorama and in order not to miss the opportunity to attack, *Valiant* remained on-station with its torpedo bow-caps open and ready to fire. At 1220, a new contact appeared. Intelligence had predicted that the *San Luis* would be in the area three hours later than this, but it was such an auspicious contact that *Valiant* went to actions stations and prepared to attack.

However, the contact was moving south, whereas the intelligence had predicted that the *San Luis* would be heading north towards its base in Mar del Plata. While following this contact, another promising contact appeared. In order to try to get a clearer picture, active sonar was used, but this only generated more confusion from the large number of spurious contacts that were gained. Later, both contacts disappeared. At 1452, another contact was picked up towards the east, heading west. At 1,600 yards, the submarine was prepared to fire but suddenly the contact split in two and passed the *Valiant* at 200 yards. Obviously, it was a biological contact.

Therefore, the *Valiant* was left empty-handed that day. Even though, it is entirely possible that one of the contacts that had been detected that day was the *San Luis*. It had arrived in the area and then turned south towards Puerto Belgrano Naval Base rather than north to the Mar del Plata base. The intelligence must have been incomplete.

The problem associated with trying to locate a Type 209 was clearly summed up by Commander Tom Le Marchand, CO of HMS *Valiant*: "Most pundits would agree that a great deal of luck would be necessary for an SSN to hold an S209 class on main motors long enough to attack it, even without the unpredictable distractions caused by fish, fishermen and amorous sea mammals."

Commander Le Marchand was not mistaken by how much luck would have been needed. According to post-conflict studies, it was found that a Type 209 submarine would be detectable with a Type 2024 towed array at ranges up to 5,000 yards when on its main motors and 50,000 yards when operating its diesel engines, and at 2,000 and 5,000 yards respectively using the hull-mounted Type 2001 sonar. These figures would be greatly reduced in shallower waters.

Had there been an opportunity for a British submarine to attack an Argentine one, the former were equipped with wire-guided Tigerfish Mk 24 torpedoes: the brand new Swiftsure-class HMS *Spartan* and HMS *Splendid* carried the Model 0 (to be used only against surface contacts or submerged submarines only at periscope depth), while HMS *Conqueror*, HMS *Valiant*, HMS *Courageous* and HMS *Onyx* carried the Model 1 which had a capability against surface and submerged targets. Both models had a maximum range of 31,600 yards (28.9 kilometres) and were fitted with both active and passive sonar. Nevertheless, the noise levels produced by the probable enemy targets, in this case the Type 209, were very low for the passive tracking head of the Tigerfish and, in shallow waters (less than 300 feet/91 metres), where an engagement would probably have occurred, it would have also had to contend with reflections from the seabed and surface when using the active sonar on board the torpedo. Worse still, the reliability of the Tigerfish was poor. The Mod 0 had a 45% reliability while the Mod 1 had a slight improvement over its predecessor of

A sequence of photographs showing a drill Mk 44 torpedo drop from a Sea King belonging to 706 NAS operational training flight in 1981. (John Osmond)

A drill torpedo Mk 44 underneath a Westland Wasp HAS.1 (XV631) in the early seventies. (Chris England)

HMS *Brilliant* (F90) in South Georgia. One of its STWS2 anti-submarine torpedo launchers with triple tubes, can be seen in the foreground. (via David Oddy)

The combination of problems in detection capacity, classification, identification and attack meant that the ability of the British submariner to deal with the threat of a modern conventional Argentine submarine was rather limited. Having all these issues in mind, the mission given to HMS *Spartan* against *San Luis* is also analysed below, as well as HMS *Conqueror*'s employment against *Santa Fe*. The British submarines´ ASW role was in no way systematic nor became their main duty. It only became a task when the opportunity, based on intelligence, presented itself and could not be missed.

54%. However, when considered as part of a system, that reliability dropped to only around 20%.

All submarines deployed to the South Atlantic also carried the old but very reliable Mk 8 mod 4 straight running torpedo, with a maximum range of 7,000 yards.

Due to these limitations, a novel tactic (or, really, an upgrade of the tactic employed by HMS *Venturer* in the Second World War to attack the German U864, the only time in the history of warfare where a submerged submarine sunk another submerged boat) against conventional submarines at periscope depth was developed in HMS *Splendid*, according to its commander, Roger Lane-Nott:

> Fire a Mark 24, drive it out at slow speed, passive, astern of the target – lagging the bearing line. When the weapon was at half target range fire a salvo of three Mark 8s using an anti-ship salvo with the weapons stepped down at depths of 36, 40 and 44 feet from aft to forward. It was hoped that the target would react to one of the four discharges giving the 8s the first go at it and then the Mark 24 would follow up as it evaded.

Anti-submarine weapons

The Task Force was equipped with three main anti-submarine weapons: the US developed Mk 46 mod 1 and Mk 44 torpedoes; and the UK made Mk 11 depth charge. The Mk 46 torpedoes were relatively modern and would run for a total of six minutes at a speed of 45 knots. If its target was within 1,000 yards of its homing head, it could carry out an autonomous attack. The Mk 44, on the other hand, was obsolete at the time of the conflict and had been removed from front line units by the US Navy in 1967. It had a speed of 30 knots and ran for six minutes, and its sonar was only capable of detecting a target at 600 yards. Both types could be launched by aircraft or fired from tubes mounted on warships (Plessey STWS-1 and STWS-2 anti-submarine launchers in triple tubes, the latter was also cleared to fire the new Sting Ray torpedo).

The IKARA was a missile system that mounted a Mk 44 torpedo. It could be fired by the ship from up to 10 nautical miles and would deploy the torpedo, which would descend to the sea surface by parachute. HMS *Bristol*, the sole Type 82 destroyer built, was the only ship deployed to the conflict area that possessed the IKARA system.

RAF Nimrods could also be armed with the new Sting Ray torpedo, manufactured by Marconi in the UK, which was also available in the

A Mk 11 depth charge (left) and a Mk 46 torpedo (right) being loaded on to a Sea King helicopter on the deck of an aircraft carrier during the war. (Royal Navy)

magazines of a limited number of escort ships in the Task Force. The Sting Ray had been recently incorporated into the Royal Navy and Royal Air Force; production had only begun in April 1981. It had a long range and a speed of 45 knots and was one of the first torpedoes to incorporate advanced microprocessors. There was a great confidence in this weapon. As the Under-Secretary of State for Defence for the Royal Navy (Mr. Keith Speed) told (again) the House of Commons on 19 June 1980:

> The new lightweight torpedo Sting Ray—designed to be launched from surface ships, helicopter and maritime patrol aircraft—will, when it enters service in the mid-1980s, be by far the most advanced weapon of its kind in the Alliance, if not the world. It will progressively replace the Mk 44 and Mk 46 torpedoes, currently in service with the Royal Navy and the RAF. Some 4,500 people are expected to be employed on Sting Ray production. It is a costly project, but I must ask whether, in the face of the growing threat, it makes sense to make a massive investment in ASW ships and aircraft unless we have the weapon with which to be certain of killing the submarine. Only Sting Ray will fulfil that requirement.

These torpedoes also had a tremendous destructive power. In the first live warhead test, carried out in October 1985 in the Mediterranean, a Sting Ray hit and destroyed its target, the submarine HMS *Porpoise*, which was moored at a depth of 65 metres. The target was so comprehensively damaged that it could not be raised to the surface to be examined.

The Mk 11 depth charge, still in use today, was only to be used against submarines at periscope depth and had a radius of damage of 30 feet (9.1 metres). If the 176lb charge exploded within ten feet (3 metres) of the submarine, it was thought that the damage it would cause would be enough to sink it. The mod 3 was the version carried during the 1982 conflict (around 1,300 weapons were converted to the mod 3 standard at the time of the war), and it had a stronger outer case to resist high-speed drops and helicopter vibrations.

A large number of torpedoes and depth charges were available against the Argentine submarines. HMS *Hermes*'s magazine was usually home to up to 48 Mk 44 torpedoes, 54 Mk 46s and 24 Mk 11 mod 3 depth charges. HMS *Invincible* carried 46 Mk 46s and 24 Mk 11s. Likewise, logistic ships also went south with a large quantity of these weapons in their magazines. For example, RFA *Olmeda* departed with 24 Mk 46s on board. Escort ships also carried their own stock of ASW weapons, either for their own use or for their helicopter(s). For example, HMS *Sheffield* carried 10 Mk 46 torpedoes when it was hit by an air launched Exocet missile on 4 May.

The Rothesay class frigates HMS *Plymouth* and HMS *Yarmouth*, were fitted with the Mk 10 Limbo ASW mortar. This was a weapon based on the Squid design used in the Second World War. These contraptions

A Sea King HAS.5 of 820 NAS at RNAS Culdrose with its weapon fit in 1981. From left to right (most relevant): a WE.177A nuclear depth charge, smoke floats, size "F" sonobuoys, 7.62mm GPMG, two Mk 46 mod 1 torpedoes, four Mk 11 mod 3 depth charges. Near the helicopter are 4.5¨ recce flares and size "A" sonobuoys. (Royal Navy)

A Royal Navy Wessex helicopter carrying a WE.177A nuclear depth charge training round. (MoD)

Table 5: British anti-submarine weapons

Anti-submarine Weapon	Max range (yds)	Weight (lbs)	Warhead weight (lbs)	Speed (knots)	Guidance
Depth charge Mk 11 mod 3	0	320	176	0	No
Anti-submarine mortar Limbo (Mk 10)	Between 400 and 1,000	390	207	0	No. Associated sonar is Type 170
Torpedo Mk 44 Mod 1	6,000	433	73	30	Active sonar
Torpedo Mk 46 mod 1	12,200	508	96	45	Active / passive sonar
Torpedo Stingray	8,750	588.5	99	45	Active / passive sonar
Nuclear depth charge WE.177A	0 (air dropped)	600	0.5 kilotons in shallow waters or 10 kilotons in deep waters	0	No

could launch a 390lb projectile to a maximum distance of 1,000 yards, set to explode at a depth between 30 and 1,200 feet (9.1 to 366 metres). They were fired in salvoes of three and would detonate at a predetermined depth (the shells were time-fuzed) with a single one of them being capable of sinking a target if exploding at 5 yards distance, however, damage could be serious on the target up to 50 yards. A ship´s magazine usually held 17 salvos (or 51 projectiles). Type 170 sonar was used to control the Limbo mortar. The commander of HMS *Yarmouth* considered the mortar to be most useful: it "...proved its worth as it was the only weapon capable of putting exploding charges onto a bottomed contact...our mortars were used extensively in the classification of the numerous "submarine" contacts gained by dippers and escorts."

No analysis of the British anti-submarine weapons deployed to the South Atlantic would be complete without mentioning the nuclear depth charge, the WE.177A.

This weapon had an adjustable yield of 0.5 or 10 kilotons. As a comparison, the Little Boy weapon dropped on Hiroshima in the Second World War had 13 kiloton yield. These would be dropped by helicopter; descend with a parachute that would be disconnected on impact with the water and then sink at a rate of 20 feet (6 metres) per second until it exploded by means of a hydrostatic fuse. The Royal Navy possessed 43 of these weapons. On leaving for the South Atlantic, the aircraft carriers *Invincible* and *Hermes* and the frigates *Broadsword* and *Brilliant* carried a still classified quantity of these weapons in their magazines. Other ships carried training versions on board, but these did not have a nuclear warhead fitted.

By May, the two frigates had transferred their weapons to logistics ships. Even so, an appreciable number of these weapons remained in the theatre of operations. Of course, it was never the intention to use these weapons against Argentine submarines, but they were retained in the Task Force as a counter to Soviet submarines should they openly intervene in the conflict. All of the nuclear weapons deployed returned to the UK after the conflict or, in other words, none were lost as a result of the sinking of Royal Navy warships by the Argentines.

Anti-submarine formations

A fleet formation is usually organised to protect its most important ships, the High Value Units (HVUs). In this conflict, the HVUs were clearly the two aircraft carriers, as described by Rear Admiral Sir John "Sandy" Woodward, the commander of Task Group 317.8: "Lose

HMS *Invincible* underway in 1982. (US Navy)

A Sting Ray torpedo armed Sea King HAS.5 of 820 NAS. Anti-submarine Sea Kings usually carried a three-digit number below the Pilot 2 cockpit window as clearly visible in this photo. The first digit refers to the ship or shore base, the second to the squadron and the third to the individual aircraft. The second and third digits are also painted on the nose and either side of the fuselage. Before the 1982 conflict white numbers were the norm, but during the war and since then, the numbers have usually been black. Commando Sea King squadrons used a different system of pennant (or side) marking: its aircraft bear just two large letters. (Royal Navy)

Invincible and the operation is severely jeopardized. Lose Hermes and the operation is over". In addition to the aircraft carriers, the other HVUs were the large logistics and troop transports ships.

The protection of the ships located in the main body was the utmost priority for the Royal Navy. So, the formation of the fleet would be organized to protect the HVUs against the three threats: surface, aerial and submarine. The escort ships were then located at positions called "station assignments" considering the threat axis – the likely direction of an enemy attack – and capabilities of the ship.

Also, during this war, an enemy submarine would be only a conventional diesel/electric one, with limited speed and endurance underwater. The attacking submarine itself would have to be aware of the Limiting Lines of Approach (LLOA) due to the fact in this scenario the speed of the submarine would usually be less than the speed of Task Force. The enemy submarine had to be within the Limiting Lines of Approach, inside the Submerged Approach Region or SAR, in order to reach an acceptable firing position (to enter the so-called Torpedo Danger Zone or TDZ). For example, a conventional submerged submarine could not start an attack movement from behind or to the side against a fast-moving warship: as it simply would not be able to get into a position to fire a torpedo against it. Taking all of this into account, it is clear that the stern of the fleet was usually empty of escorts or helicopters.

As a young pilot from 826 NAS explained:

> Believe it or not, sinking the *San Luis* was not our main aim, but sanitizing the waters ahead of the Carrier Battle Group to ensure neither carrier was not [sic] sunk by the *San Luis*. ASW in that form was a defensive strategy. A diesel/electric submarine has a very narrow channel of attack on a moving ship and our job was to keep that clear of threats.

Back to the formation, the first line of protection for the HVUs were the Type 22 frigates. These were armed with the modern short-range Sea Wolf missile. At the time, this was possibly the only Western missile capable of shooting down a sea-skimming missile such as the Exocet. Further out were the escorts whose primary mission was anti-submarine. These were usually the Type 21 frigates of which there would generally be two or three at a radius of seven miles from the main body. These ships would have their helicopters on anti-submarine configuration at different levels of alert. Further still, Sea King helicopters would each occupy some of the nine 40° sectors at a distance between 12 and 20 nautical miles from the HVUs.

ACCIDENT

Parent unit/Ship Squadron Place Date	Aircraft type Serial no.	Crew
HMS HERMES 826 Naval Air Squadron At Sea 12 May 1982	SEA KING HAS5 ZA132	Sub Lt K B SUTTON (U) Sub Lt A J MOSS (U) Lt Cdr J S CHANDLER (U) LACMN P W COOMBES (U)

1. The aircraft was in its seventh ASW hover of the sortie having been airbrone for 1½ hours. Whilst in a 60 foot hover, VMC with sea state 6 and the sonar body lowered to 200 feet a large torque split occurred.

2. From hover torques of 78%-78% the No 2 ECU ran down to zero and the No 1 ECU ran up to 140%, while Nr decayed rapidly to 85%.

3. The radio altimeter indicated the weave height as 20 feet and the pilot attempted transition after the sonar cable was cut, but the aircraft struck a wave crest, flew across the trough and settled on the next crest. When the aircraft reached the following trough the tail rotor struck with a loud bang and the aircraft yawed rapidly to starboard. Both SSLs were pulled to 'shot off' and the aircraft rolled over to port as the yaw stopped.

4. All four crew members evacuated the aircraft and were recovered by helicopter after about 20 minutes in the water.

5. The cause of the accident was the loss of power on No 2 ECU probably caused by fuel starvation or by computer malfunction.

Accident report. Loss of Sea King HAS.5 ZA132 (826 NAS) on 12 May 1982. (Royal Navy)

The crew of Sea King HAS.5 XZ573 belonging to 826 NAS was rescued by another Sea King helicopter, of 820 NAS, when it crashed on 17 May. This was the second crash in a few days, and the Squadron scrapbook reflects it! (MoD)

A post-war view of Sea King HAS.5 XV655 (coded 265) operating from HMS *Hermes*. XV655 deployed down south with 814 NAS, based on the aircraft carrier HMS *Illustrious*, shortly after the hostilities ended. The MAD antenna is clearly visible on starboard sponson in this photograph. (Royal Navy)

Generally, the sector ahead of the fleet, in the line of advance, would be occupied by a Sea King. Often, if the situation required or intelligence suggested it, there would be a Ripple 3 mission carried out by each of the carrier ASW squadrons. This involved each carrier based Naval Air Squadron (820 and 826) having two Sea Kings on ASW stations and a third either in transit to or from the scene. This would mean that there would be up to six Sea Kings operating in the ASW screen at the same time. The average flight time of each helicopter would be around three and a half hours. Not an easy task, according to Lieutenant Steve George, from 820 NAS deployed on *Invincible*:

> A 'Ripple 3' meant three lines on the flypro, each filled by an aircraft. Depending on the range at which the ASW screen was required (we're talking 'pinging' with active sonar here), this would generate two aircraft out on the screen, with the third aircraft outbound or inbound. When an aircraft had to be changed (either unserviceable or it ran out of hours) then we'd have to generate a fourth aircraft which would normally launch before the aircraft being pulled out of the 'ripple' returned. We always kept a 'Spare on Deck' (SOD) primed and ready in case one of the aircraft went U/S [unserviceable] on the deck.
>
> In 1982, shortly after we set sail for Ascension, our squadron was tasked to support not only a 'Ripple 3', but also an additional line for Surface Search. This line required more than one aircraft, as the aircraft taking over often had to launch before the other SS aircraft came back.

The Sea Kings would generally be armed with Mk 46 anti-submarine torpedoes and/or Mk 11 depth charges. The numbers would vary, but usually they would carry one or two torpedoes and one or two depth charges per aircraft.

The anti-submarine task was very challenging for the machines and the crews. 820 NAS Pilot, Lieutenant B.A. Jones thought:

> As we were ripple flying, it was very much a "Groundhog Day" routine. Get woken up, eat, brief, fly, debrief, eat, sleep repeat. Often when woken up we had no idea if it was night or day
>
> It was boring, tedious and repetitive, enlivened only by the occasional contact that required further investigation (usually by dropping a depth charge) or the occasional torpedo drop. We relied entirely on the accuracy and reliability of the Sea King AFCS/Auto-hover (Doppler and Cable mode), which was exceptional. By June we were all very fatigued; it was a constant battle to avoid falling asleep and I'm confident that at some points in the flight (hover) the whole crew were briefly dozing! The weather was often appalling, so even by day a lot of the flight would IFR/IMC. We flew in conditions well below peacetime minima and made many PVA (Poor Visibility Approaches) recoveries. This strain added to the general fatigue.

Therefore, it was not at all unexpected that some accidents took place. On 12 May the first accident occurred in which Sea King HAS.5 ZA132 of 826 NAS was lost. It was in a stationary hover at 60 feet (18 metres) with the sonar deployed beneath at a depth of 200 feet (60 metres). This was the seventh dip of the sortie. At that moment, the helicopter suffered an abrupt loss of power and finished up contacting the surface of the sea. The four crew members managed to get out of the aircraft and were rescued shortly thereafter.

A second HAS.5 of 826 NAS was lost on the 17 May when XZ573, while on an ASW sortie, had a failure of the radar altimeter on a dark night with no visible horizon. The pilot became disoriented and the helicopter was damaged when it inadvertently made contact with the sea. The crew was rescued, but the helicopter, that was floating on the surface, was later sunk with naval gunfire as its recovery was considered to be too risky. This was partly due to the potential presence of an Argentine submarine and the also the possibility that the depth charges being carried by the helicopter might explode during recovery. They finally exploded when the helicopter sank!

Furthest out were the picket ships. These would typically be Type 42 destroyers or, later, the Type 82 HMS *Bristol*. Their long-range radars and Sea Dart anti-air missiles were the first line of warning and defence, especially against Argentine aircraft.

This would complete the formation of the fleet.

Table 6: Anti-submarine mission hours flown by Task Force helicopters (April, May and June 1982)

Helicopter model	ASW hours April	ASW hours May	ASW hours June	
Lynx	51	70	49	
Sea King HAS.2	32	169	51	
Sea King HAS.5	624	2,371	1,066	
Wasp	4	30	4	
Wessex HAS.3	21	60	0	
TOTALS	**732**	**2,700**	**1,170**	**4,602**

The coordination of all these units was conducted from one of the aircraft carriers. A ship of this size was needed to exercise command and control and to provide ASW helicopters and Sea Harriers for area air defence.

British submarines operated independently of surface forces and under the control of a separate command. Therefore, measures were taken to prevent blue-on-blue incidents. According to the Flag Officer Submarines (FOSM):

> mutual separation from surface and air ASW units was achieved by defining, and periodically updating, an ASW weapons tight boundary between Task Force operating areas and submarine patrol areas (SPAs). A Buffer Zone, normally of 30 to 50nm in depth, was maintained between the ASW weapons tight boundary and the nearest SPA.

At the same time, the fleet constantly carry out the old and basic anti-submarine manoeuvre known as the zigzag. This involved making continual and random changes in direction and the maximum speed available.

The commander of one of the escorts, Captain David Pentreath (*Plymouth's* CO) summarises the ASW posture: "The ASW posture in the Total Exclusion Zone was overt, relying on the speed and continual manoeuvring of the two carriers to provide self-protection behind a screen of dippers and escorts."

Also, according to Commander William Howard, Task Group Commander's ASW Staff Officer throughout under Rear Admiral Sandy Woodward:

> The Organization of ASW Defence was conducted using NATO doctrine and dispositions and tactics informed by threat intelligence. The distances involved meant that Maritime Patrol Aircraft (MPA) did not usually form part of a defence in depth. Similarly, the threat analysis meant that the SSNs were rarely used in the ASW role. ASW helicopters (Sea Kings) usually formed the first line of defence and were occasionally also used in the MPA role. The second line of defence were the frigates and destroyers.
>
> Surface Attack Units (SAUs) comprising frigates/destroyers, support ships (as aircraft re-fuelling and re-arming platforms) and ASW helicopters were formed to combat specific threats and to conduct specific operations.

The last line in protection against an Argentine torpedo came in the form of the Type 182 towed torpedo decoy. They were prone to having problems with the cables that attached them to the ship they were towed from, or being damaged in use, for example from water ingress. Many of the decoys were lost at sea from these problems. According to Captain David Pentreath, *Plymouth's* CO:

> Without doubt the biggest single headache was the unreliability of Sonar Decoy 182. This vital piece of equipment … had at one time two Senior Ratings working continuously 24 hours a day just to keep the inboard body/cable serviceable. From reading signals, it became apparent that 182 was proving equally troublesome in other ships…many hours were spent, in darkness on a heaving quarterdeck in poor weather conditions, recovering, repairing and streaming the 182 due to a design defect which had been common knowledge since 1979.

Nevertheless, British pre-conflict studies had concluded that the SST-4 torpedo had a 95% effectiveness against targets that were not protected by decoy if the torpedo was launched from no more than 5 kilometres distance. It was thought that, in the words of the report that "the decoy 182 is likely to be very effective in reducing the SST-4 homing system hit probability from about 95 % to a much lower figure which cannot be accurately quantified". For this reason, it had been recommended to always deploy the decoy.

Type 22 frigate HMS *Brilliant* (F90) in 1995. (US Navy)

Westland Sea King HAS.5 XZ918/020 (820 Naval Air Squadron based on HMS *Invincible*) with its GEC-Plessey Type 195M dipping sonar deployed, in May 1982. (Artwork by Javier 'Javo' Ruberto)

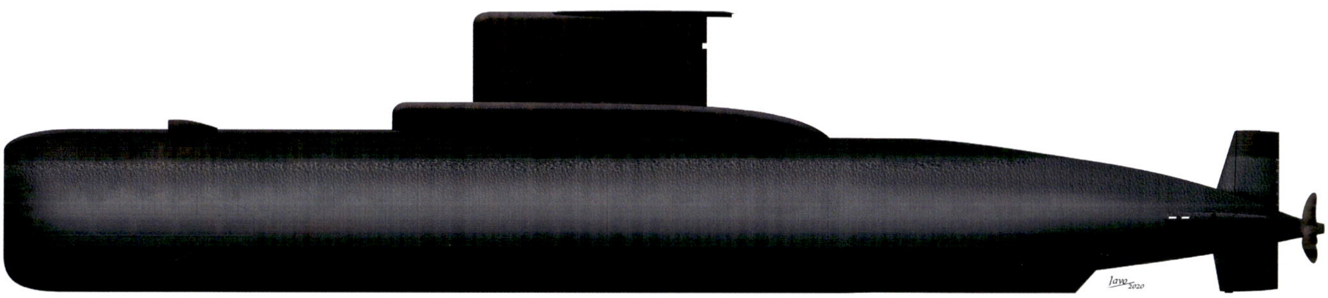

ARA *San Luis* (S-32) Type 209/1200 class submarine, in May 1982. (Artwork by Javier 'Javo' Ruberto)

ARA *Santa Fe* (S-21) a Balao class submarine modernized to a GUPPY II standard, in April 1982. (Artwork by Javier 'Javo' Ruberto)

Westland Lynx HAS.2 XZ729/342 (815 Naval Air Squadron, *Brilliant* Flight), armed with a single Mk 46 torpedo, in early May 1982. The MAD bird is on the other side of the aircraft and not visible. XZ729 strafed submarine ARA *Santa Fe* with machine gun fire on 25 April 1982 and was seriously damaged on 25 May 1982 by a bomb, while operating from HMS *Broadsword*. (Artwork by Javier 'Javo' Ruberto)

Westland Wessex HAS.3 XP142/406, known as "Humphrey" (737 Naval Air Squadron, *Antrim* Flight) armed with two Mk 11 mod 3 depth charges, in April 1982. Humphrey, crewed by Lieutenant Commander Ian Stanley, Sub-Lieutenant Stewart Cooper, Lieutenant Chris Parry and Petty Officer Aircrewman David Fitzgerald, fired the first shots of the Task Force on 25 April 1982 when it dropped the depth charges on the submarine *Santa Fe*. (Artwork by Javier 'Javo' Ruberto)

Westland Wasp HAS.1 XS527/434 (829 Naval Air Squadron, *Endurance* Flight) armed with two Nord AS.12 missiles, in April 1982. On 25 April 1982, this helicopter, with Lt Cdrs Tony Ellerbeck and David Wells onboard, fired six missiles against submarine ARA *Santa Fe* and scored three hits. (Artwork by Javier 'Javo' Ruberto)

Hawker Siddeley Nimrod MR2P XV234 (201 Squadron RAF) in late June 1982. XV234 had the artwork "Jane" applied to the port side forward fuselage, with the annotation "201 Sqn Crew 1, Senior Nimrod Combat Crew South Atlantic" written underneath. On 18 August 1982, 201 Sqn Crew 1, flying in XV234, was the last Kinloss crew to leave Ascension Island and returned to Kinloss via Gibraltar on 19 August, marking the end of Nimrod involvement in Operation Corporate. (Artwork by Javier 'Javo' Ruberto)

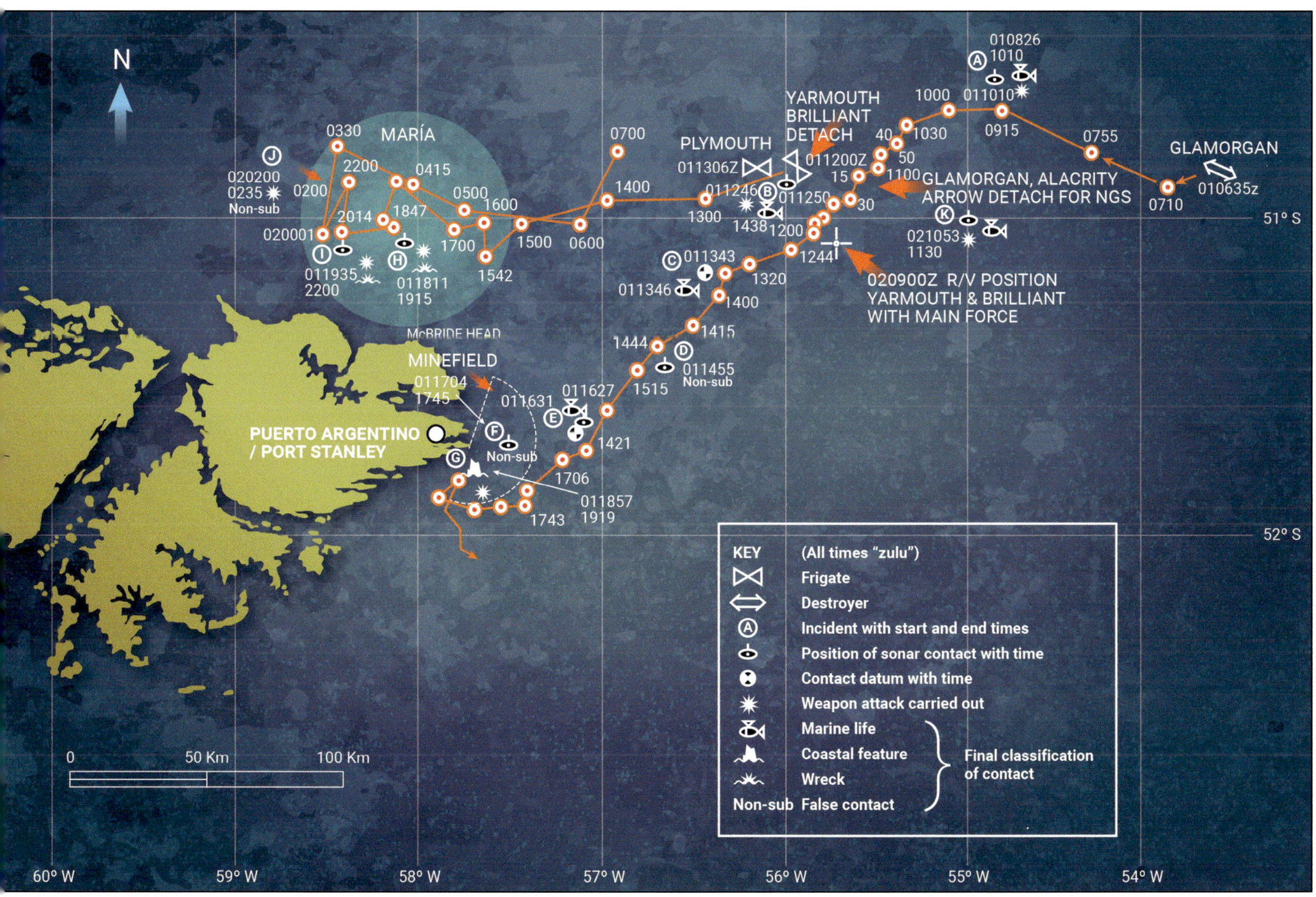

UK anti-submarine actions, 1 May 1982. (Map by Guillermo Messina)

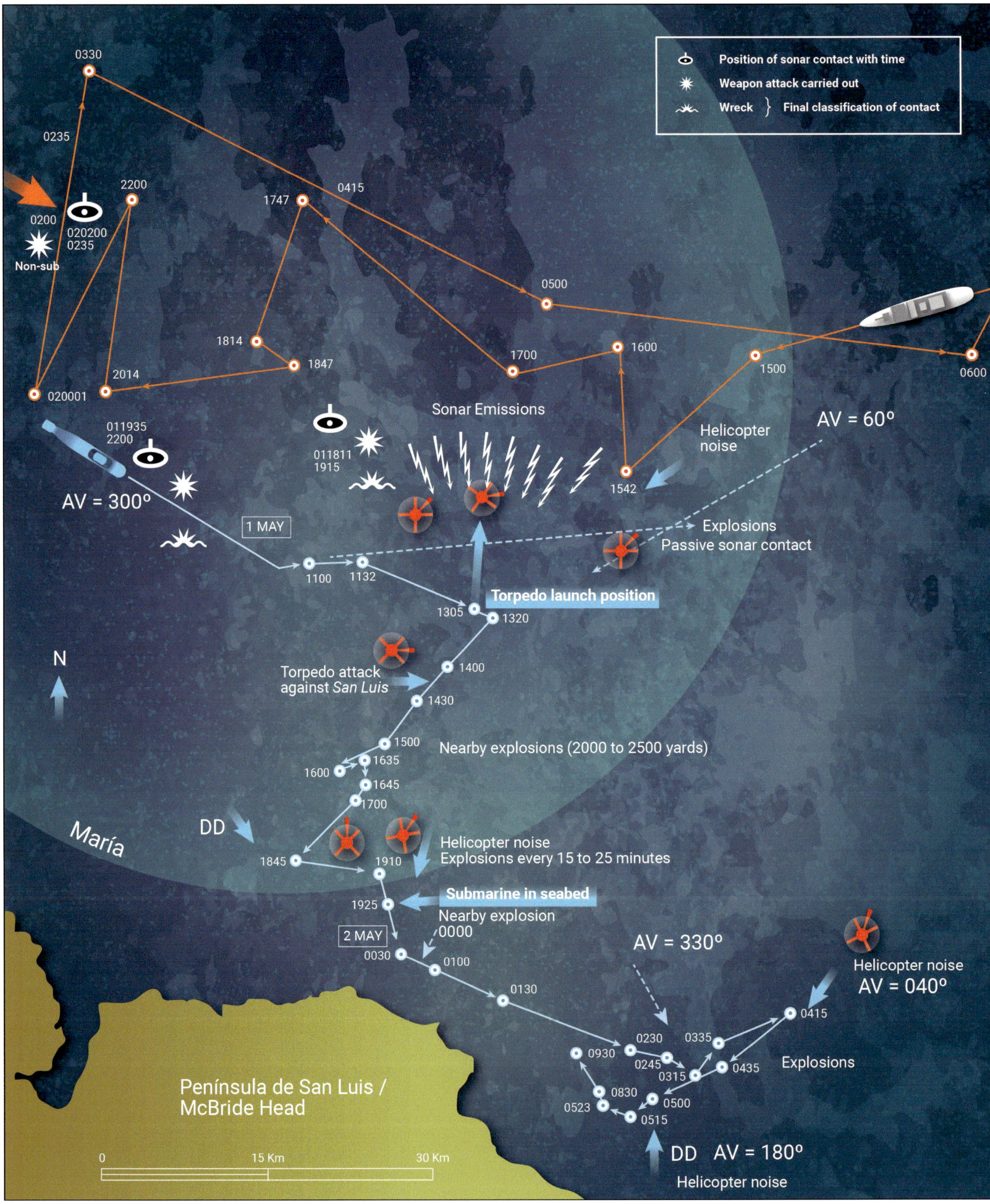

British anti-submarine effort vs ARA *San Luis*. 1 May 1982. (Map by Guillermo Messina)

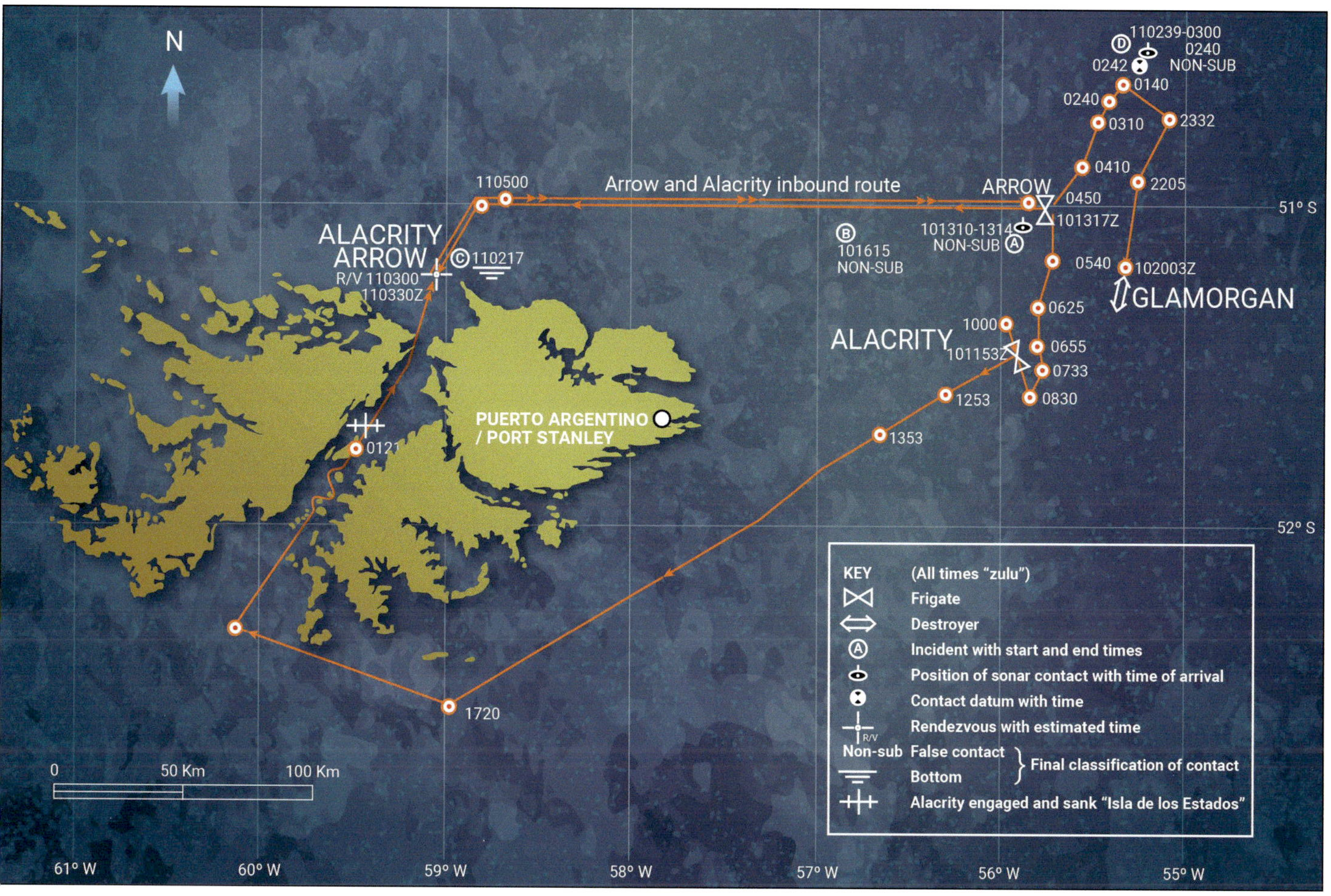

HMS *Alacrity*, HMS *Arrow* and anti-submarine incidents. 10/11 May 1982. (Map by Guillermo Messina)

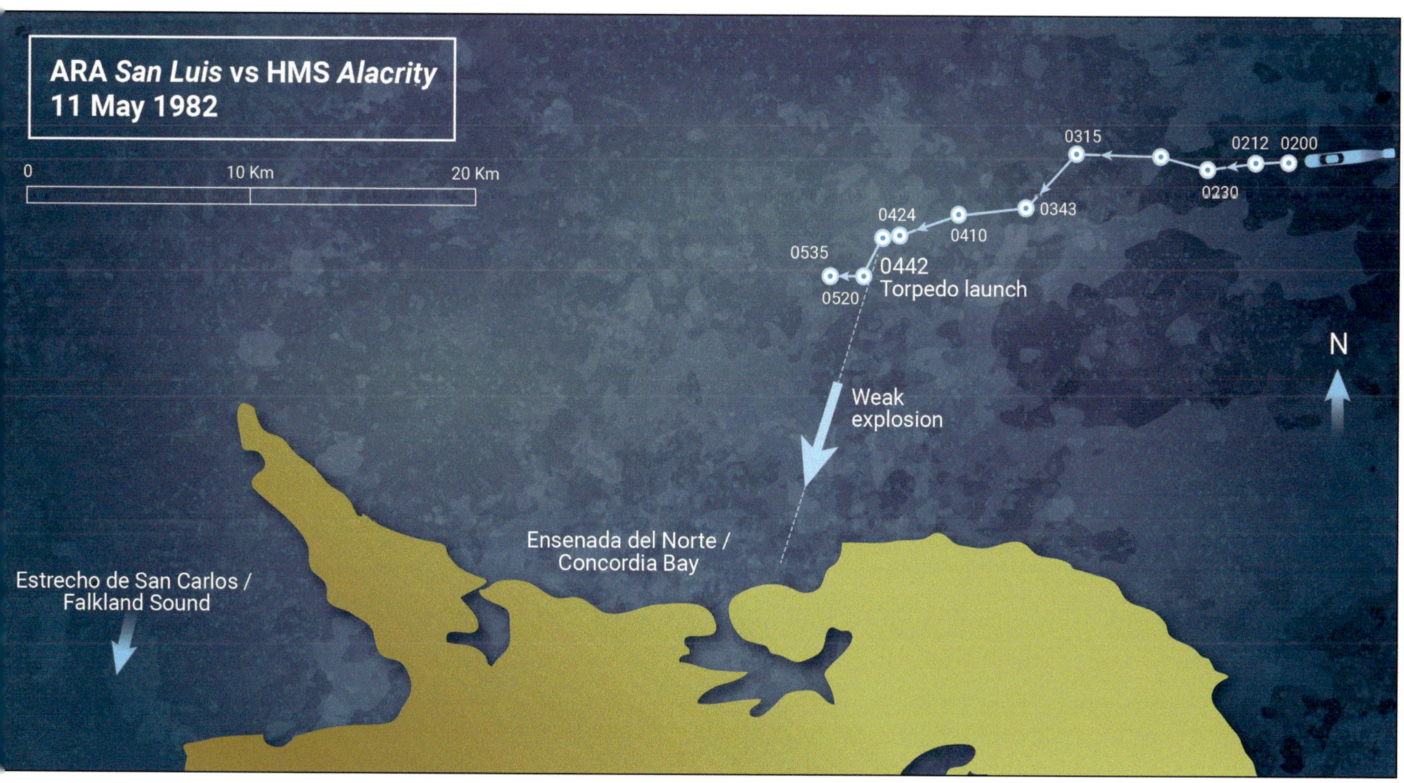

ARA *San Luis* vs HMS *Alacrity*. 11 May 1982. (Map by Guillermo Messina)

Submarine ARA *Santa Fe*. 25 April 1982. (Map by Guillermo Messina)

Argentine submarine patrol areas. (Map by Guillermo Messina)

A typical circular formation used by the Royal Navy during the war. From the center to the top: The HVUs and at least one Type 22 frigate; the Type 21 frigates and, in the outer ring, Sea King ASW helicopters. (Diagram by Guillermo Messina)

HMS *Yarmouth* (F101). (Ken Griffiths)

An aerial view of Type 42 class destroyer HMS *Glasgow* (D88) during NATO Exercise DISTANT DRUM 83. The exercise was carried out in the Mediterranean Sea, from 17 to 27 May. (US Navy)

Merchant ships and vessels of the Royal Fleet Auxiliary that took part in the conflict, for the same reason, deployed the older Unifoxer decoy with which they had hastily been fitted (some warships had Type 182 and Unifoxer attached). In one case, the crew of the CS *Iris* made a make-shift decoy from objects that they found onboard the ship. The effectiveness of this artefact was fortunately never tested.

Contact Classification, attack criteria and its many problems

Before continuing, it is worth clarifying the classification system, as used by the Royal Navy, for categorising presumed submerged contacts according to their degree of confidence:

1. CERTSUB – (certain submarine) A contact has been sighted and positively identified as a submarine.
2. PROBSUB – (probable submarine) A contact that displays strong evidence of being a submarine
3. POSSUB – The classification (possible submarine) is given to a contact on which available information indicates the likely presence of a submarine, however there is insufficient evidence to justify a higher classification. POSSUB is always followed by an assessment of the confidence level: LOW CONFIDENCE (1 or 2) or HIGH CONFIDENCE (3 or 4). The launch criteria for ASW weapons were at least POSSUB HIGH 3 for a torpedo and POSSUB LOW 1 for a depth charge and anti-submarine mortars.
4. NONSUB – This condition is indicated when a visual sighting or the sound/radar evaluation is satisfied that the contact is not a submarine.

Once a contact was established, the unit that had discovered the contact would become the on-scene commander. It would be required to pass on, as soon as possible, its classification to the rest of the fleet. This task required, on average, around 25 minutes from initial contact to classification. The best option to aid with the classification was to use the modern Type 2016 sonar that was fitted to the Type 22 frigates HMS *Broadsword* and *Brilliant*.

Unfortunately, these ships were in demand as close escorts for the aircraft carriers as they were fitted with the lethal Sea Wolf missiles. Therefore, they were often unable to abandon their station close to the carrier they were tasked with protecting. The only other ship that took part in the conflict that was fitted with a Type 2016 was HMS *Andromeda*. However, this ship did not arrive in the theatre of operations until towards the end of May, when the submarine threat was already much diminished.

A rather more violent and simplistic method used to classify submerged contacts was the use of a depth charge, which was done on several occasions. They were used in an attempt to separate a NONSUB from a POSSUB. This was achieved by monitoring the reaction of the submerged contact following a close by explosion. This "get a weapon in the water" method was expensive, but highly effective. Also, as previously mentioned, the Magnetic Anomaly Detector, which was only fitted to a few helicopters, were not useful.

False contacts were a constant, even for those with the best equipment and personnel. Certainly, the lack of experience in the conditions and environment of the South Atlantic affected the British anti-submarine capability. It is also worth recognising the fact that, as the conflict progressed, the frequency of the spurious contacts decreased.

The errors in the classification of contacts can be explained, to a degree, by the submarine paranoia that occurred within the British Task Force, especially during the first days of war. A good example of this was the many submarine and torpedo sightings reported in the aftermath of the successful attack on HMS *Sheffield* by Argentine aircraft of the 4 May, in the vicinity of the burning ship. None of these sightings could have been real and, according to Task Force 317.8 War Diary: "post incident analysis assessed the torpedo reports to be probably Gemini engines being used by *Sheffield* to fight the fire from outboard, and sonar contacts to be non-subs."

Table 7: Anti-submarine attacks during Operation Corporate								
Date	**Time**	**Attacking unit**	**Classification level**	**Torpedo Mk 46**	**Torpedo Mk 44**	**Depth Charge Mk 11**	**Limbo Mortar (salvoes)**	**Notes**
24 April	No info	Sea King 820 NAS	POSSUB 3	1				Later classified as whale
25 April	1832	Sea King	POSSUB 3	1		1		Later classified as whale
25 April	0854	Wessex (*Antrim* flight)	CERTSUB			2		ARA *Santa Fe* attack
	0900	Lynx (*Brilliant* flight)	CERTSUB	1				ARA *Santa Fe* attack
26 April	No info	Sea King 820 NAS	POSSUB 1			1		
01 May	1003	*Brilliant*	POSSUB 2	2				Torpedoes exploded when entering the sea surface
	1300	*Plymouth*	POSSUB 4				1	
	1310	Sea King	POSSUB 4		1			
	1900	*Glamorgan*			1			
		Wasp (*Yarmouth* flight)						
		Lynx (*Brilliant* flight)						
	1500 to 2200 (action against ARA *San Luis*)	*Yarmouth*	No info	3	3	3	7	*Yarmouth* fired 14 mortar bombs this day
		Brilliant						
		Sea King 826 NAS						
02 May	0235	*Yarmouth*					1	
	1100	*Yarmouth*	POSSUB 2				4	*Yarmouth* fired 10 mortar bombs this day
04 May	0045	*Yarmouth*	POSSUB (no further info)				1	
	0452	Helicopter	POSSUB 1			1		
	1451	*Glasgow*	Visual	1				From here to the end of the day, attacks related to sightings near HMS *Sheffield*
	After 1420	Sea King 826 NAS	No info	3		2		
	After 1420	Sea King 824 NAS	No info	1		2		
	1530	*Yarmouth*	No info				1	
	1549	*Yarmouth*	No info				1	
	1601	*Yarmouth*	No info				1	
	1612	*Yarmouth*	No info				1	
	1745	Wasp (*Yarmouth* flight)	No info		1			Torpedo malfunction
	1808	*Yarmouth*	No info				4	*Yarmouth* fired 25 mortar bombs this day

Table 7: Anti-submarine attacks during Operation Corporate

	No info	Sea King 820 NAS	POSSUB 1			1		Depth charge did not detonate
	No info	Sea King 820 NAS	POSSUB 1			1		
	No info	Sea King 820 NAS	POSSUB 2	1				
	2003	Sea King 820 NAS	POSSUB 3			1		
	2055	Sea King 820 NAS	POSSUB 3	3		2		
	2153	Helicopter	POSSUB 3	1				Possibly *Arrow* flight
05 May	No info	Lynx (*Brilliant* flight)	No info	1				Near wreck of *Sheffield*
07 May	0742	Lynx	*Coventry* ESM			1		
09 May	0005	Sea Lynx (*Alacrity* flight)	*Alacrity* doppler radar	1				Seaweed was detected in the attack area
11 May	1630	Wessex (*Antrim* flight)	POSSUB 4	1				
12 May	No info	Sea King 820 NAS	POSSUB 1			2		
13 May	0457	Helicopter	POSSUB 1			2		
	1108	Helicopter	No info			1		
	1121	Helicopter	No info			1		
	1908	Helicopter	POSSUB 1			1		Possibly the helicopter was of 820 NAS (it cannot be confirmed)
16 May	Around 1515	Helicopter	POSSUB 1			3		
	Night hours	Sea King 826 NAS	No info			2		One of the depth charges did not work
17 May	1250	Sea King 824 NAS	POSSUB 1			2		One of the depth charges did a surface burst
21 May	No info	Sea King 826 NAS	No info			1		
	No info	Sea King 820 NAS	POSSUB 1			1		
22 May	0247 to 0255	Sea King 826 NAS	No info			2		
23 May	0410	*Ambuscade*	POSSUB 3	1				
	1259	Sea King 826 NAS	POSSUB 1			2		
24 May	1147	Helicopter	No info			1		Possibly the helicopter was of 820 NAS (it cannot be confirmed)
	2138	Helicopter	No info			1		
	2143	Helicopter	No info			1		
	No info	Sea King 826 NAS	No info	1		1		
26 May	No info	Sea King 826 NAS	No info			1		
	No info	Sea King 820 NAS	POSSUB 1			1		

Table 7: Anti-submarine attacks during Operation Corporate

30 May	No info	Sea King 826 NAS	No info			1		
02 Jun	0138	*Cardiff*	POSSUB 3	1				
	No info	Sea King 820 NAS	POSSUB 1			1		
03 Jun	0300	Helicopter	No info			1		
11 Jun	0845	Sea King 820 NAS	POSSUB 3			1		Later classified as marine life
12 Jun	No info	Sea King 826 NAS	No info			1		
	TOTALS			24	6	49	22 (70 projectiles)	

A good description of the chaos that ensued following the attack is encapsulated in the account of Chief Petty Officer Arthur Gold, who was on board HMS *Arrow*, a Type 21 frigate that went to the aid of HMS *Sheffield*:

> The first time we tried to help the *Sheffield* fight her fires, we had just come alongside when an enemy submarine fired torpedoes at us. The skipper went full ahead on the engines and commenced a zigzag evasion course. One of the torpedoes missed us and the other was seduced on to our Unifoxer, which we had prudently towed astern of us.
>
> The sub fired twice more as we tried to go alongside the *Sheffield*, but we managed to side-step them each time. At one stage in the proceedings our echo-sounding gear produced a clear drawing of the sub as it passed beneath us, did a U-turn and passed beneath us once again. At about this time the *Yarmouth* arrived on the scene and went after the sub like a terrier after a rat. Over the next two hours she gave it salvo after salvo from her Limbo depth bomb mortars, and finally produced a spreading pool of oil with masses of air bubbles at its centre.

Indeed, *Yarmouth* also detected the submerged contact and, according to its commander, "for the following hour we fought a "submarine". Sea Kings were sent to assist and made contact which confirmed our contacts. Torpedo Hydrophone Effect (HE) was heard, torpedoes tracks were seen and reported…"

Obviously, the pool of oil described by Chief Petty Officer Arthur Gold could not have existed or could only have been whale oil. What *is* certain is that the only sure underwater impact that day had taken place at 1451z when HMS *Glasgow* fired a Mk 46 torpedo which exploded noisily moments later. It was soon realised by the crew that the torpedo had hit the destroyer's own Type 182 torpedo decoy, which had been left deployed in the water during the frenzied activity that followed the attack on the *Sheffield*.

During the conflict, a total of 233 anti-submarine defensive actions took place. It could be said that the anti-submarine warfare operations carried out during Operation Corporate was mainly of defensive nature: the aim being to prevent their own assets from coming under attack from a submarine. As a crew member (Pilot) of 820 NAS, Lieutenant B.A. Jones affirmed: "The value of an ASW screen lies in its deterrent capability, and therefore the screen in the South Atlantic can be said to have been 100 per cent effective: no ships of the force suffered damage by submarines."

Despite this purely defensive ASW strategy, the Royal Navy surface fleet did go on the offensive on two occasions. The first of these was on 1 May when a search attack unit (SAU) detached from the main body of the Task Force in order to try to locate and destroy the *San Luis*. We will look at this in more detail later.

The second was on 5 May when, for 48 hours, a passive (JEZEBEL) sonobuoy barrier was sown and maintained in an effort to intercept the *San Luis* which, thanks to a rather accurate intelligence report, was known to be heading towards the smouldering remains of HMS *Sheffield*.

This mission was carried out by the Sea Kings of 820 and 826 NAS, with the assistance of a Lynx helicopter, whose job was to perform electronic surveillance of the area of operations with the intention of detecting any possible electronic emissions coming from their quarry, principally radio transmissions.

According to Lieutenant Commander Ralph John Wykes-Sneyd CO of 820 NAS:

> As *Sheffield* lay dead in the water, her fires having been put out, intelligence indicated that the Argentines′ small 209 submarines had been instructed to torpedo any ships coming to tow *Sheffield* away. I deployed two anti-submarine helicopters around her, and above this scene there were two Harriers on CAP.

No contact was made. COFUERSUB annulled the order given to the *San Luis* long before it reached the area where the *Sheffield* was located.

5
"BRUISER LOOSE"

THE *SANTA FE*: 19 APRIL TO ITS END

The *Santa Fe*, from 19-21 April while en route to South Georgia (Georgias del Sur), had to battle through a storm. This left it with problems with the fibreglass skin of the fin and on the upper part of the superstructure. Now, having had its hydro-dynamic lines disrupted, the submarine was even noisier than when it had left port.

Capitán de Corbeta Horacio Alberto Bicain, the submarine's commander, recalled: "We came up against a really big storm which was the origin of part of the skin of the fin becoming detached. Even at a depth of 50 metres we could feel the storm."

A short time later, the *Santa Fe* headed directly for Grytviken (heading to 160°), where the main Argentine forces in the remote islands were located. It had received orders from COFUERSUB via radio to complete the mission sooner than planned as the British forces were closing on the island. Its crew was instructed, however, to take "extreme measures to avoid detection", but was also asked to acknowledge receipt of the message and report their position.

Bicain carried out the order as instructed even though he thought it was a very bad idea to use the VHF radio. He sent an enciphered message on 23 April at 1015z:

> TAKING DIRECT COURSE. DELAYED BY PROBLEMS WITH ENGINES (NOW REPAIRED) AND WEATHER. DAMAGE TO FIN, SKIN DETACHED AND LOSE, ESM LIMITATIONS. AZIMUTH INDICATOR NON-OPERATIONAL, ESTIMATED ARRIVAL AT GRY 241100 HRS. POSITION 230715 LATITUDE 49°54´S LONGITUDE 38°45´W.

During the first minutes of the 24 April, while he was approaching South Georgia (Georgias del Sur), he was informed by COFUERSUB that there were British units 40 miles to the north of Grytviken and that these units could be a Task Group that was preparing to take military action against the Argentine forces on the island. This information had come from reconnaissance flights made by the Argentine Air Force with Boeing 707 and Hercules C-130 aircraft.

These ships formed part of TG 317.9 and had been tasked with recovering the islands for the Crown under Operation Paraquet. The vessels involved were the destroyer HMS *Antrim* (Captain Brian Young), the frigate HMS *Plymouth* (Captain David Pentreath) and the Antarctic survey ship HMS *Endurance* (Captain Nick Barker). They were accompanied by the logistics ships RFA *Tidespring* and RFA *Brambleleaf*.

Likewise, and unknown to COFUERSUB and the crew of the *Santa Fe*, from 18 April the nuclear-powered attack submarine, HMS *Conqueror* (Commander Chris Wreford-Brown) was also located somewhere in the vicinity. During the last hours of 19 April, *Conqueror* had received the permission to attack any Argentine warship or auxiliaries, including submarines. More specifically, any non-nuclear-powered submarine should be presumed to be enemy and attacked.

British intelligence had already intercepted the transmission of the orders for the *Santa Fe* to approach South Georgia and *Conqueror* was waiting for it. The commander had had two Tigerfish Mod 1 torpedoes loaded in its tubes, which was the only weapon it possessed for use against a submerged target, even with dubious results. While waiting (and after carrying out a reconnaissance off South Georgia´s northern coastline), it had a series of detections, most of which could not be classified one way or another. The most interesting event happened on 21 May, at 1604. *Conqueror*´s CO (Chris Wreford-Brown):

> While deep, an interesting two pens HF sonar contact was detected and classified as a possible submarine contact. This was investigated both actively and passively, with bow caps open and ready to fire. However, no positive echo was achieved and insufficient passive characteristics were obtained to warrant firing a Mark 24 torpedo. Since the weather was rough at the time, the contact could not have been a surface vessel, and, reluctantly, it was classified as probably BIO.

HMS *Conqueror* on the surface near South Georgia. Behind are HMS *Antrim* (left) and HMS *Plymouth* (right). 26 April 1982. (Royal Navy)

In the early hours of 24 April, *Conqueror* received the message COR 099. This confirmed that there was a submarine threat in the area and that it should counteract it, taking up a patrol position some 120 nautical miles to the northeast of South Georgia. However, seven hours later message COR 102 was received, which informed them that the enemy submarine should be found to the north of Cumberland Bay (Bahía Guardia Nacional).

Armed with this new information, *Conqueror*'s commander decided to proceed at high speed to the east and, once in position, search in the direction of Cumberland. Wreford-Brown had the impression that the *Santa Fe* would snorkel and recharge its batteries at night and, therefore, they would have an opportunity to find and attack it on the night of the 25th, or the small hours of the 26th.

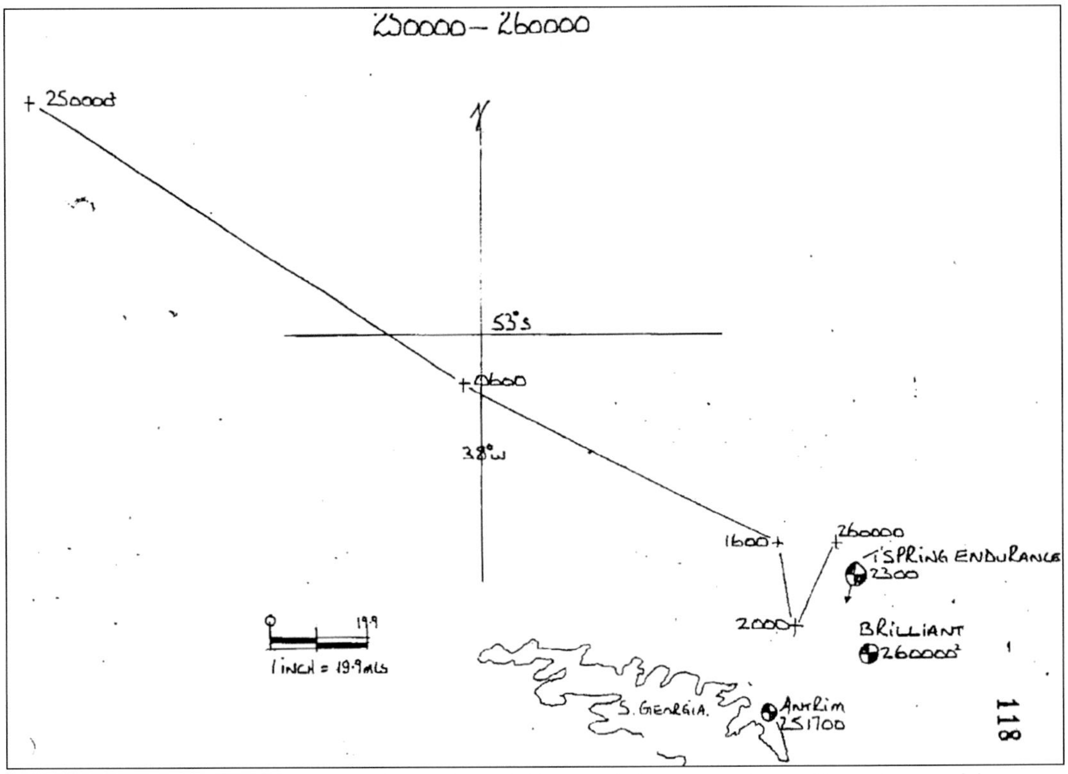

HMS *Conqueror*'s movements to South Georgia. The chart shows also the position of some of the other ships of the Task Group assembled to assault the islands. HMS *Conqueror*'s commander was concerned about ARA *Santa Fe* but also about friendly fire! However, the daily report of Sunday 25 April 1982 ends with "A good day for the RN!" (HMS *Conqueror* Report of Proceedings)

Finally, late on 24 April, communication COR 106 was received, which was the intercepted message sent by the *Santa Fe*. It had been a bad idea for the *Santa Fe* to send the message, as it had been intercepted by the SIGINT (Signals Intelligence) capable HMS *Endurance*. Captain Nick Barker wrote about it: "At 1430 our ´listeners´ intercepted a HF transmission which we believed came from an Argentine submarine. The strength of the signal seemed to indicate that the submarine was within a hundred miles of us."

The Royal Navy, after the communication was deciphered in the UK and sent back to the South Atlantic, was now fully aware of the *Santa Fe* being in the Area of Operations, its position and its Estimate Time of Arrival.

According to Captain David Pentreath, *Plymouth*´s CO:

> Much against the predictions of the ´pundits´ the Argentinians chose to deploy the Guppy *Santa Fe* in the reinforcement of South Georgia, and might have seriously jeopardised operations in that area had it not been for a timely HF intercept by HMS *Endurance* of transmissions on a known submarine operating frequency which alerted us to the presence of an enemy submarine assessed to be within 100 miles of the force.

The *Santa Fe*, from the early hours of the 24th, was heading south. It had taken a direct course to a point 70 nautical miles to the north of Cape North, not far from the most westerly point on the island, and from there was transiting towards the island at low speed.

Having approached the island, the submarine travelled along the north coast, very closely (3,000 to 4,000 yards from land) in order to avoid being detected by sonar, until it reached Robertson Point, where it surfaced. After a scare following picking up an unclear propeller sound, the submarine continued with its journey and entered Bahía Guardia Nacional. ARA *Santa Fe* had somehow managed to avoid the trap that had been set for it.

It was, by now, the middle of the night. The submarine's commander, not knowing the area and with a low-resolution radar, preferred not to get too close to the jetty of Grytviken. Once there, and with the assistance of a British Antarctic Survey (BAS) launch that had been requisitioned, the passengers and their cargo were unloaded. In the early hours of 25 April, the unloading was complete, and the submarine made its way to the entrance of the bay.

The plan was to get as far away as possible on the surface and then submerge in deeper waters and remain there during the day, and at night surface and enter one of the many bays or coves on the north coast of the island. This would enable the submarine to fully recharge its batteries, which were then at around 75%, and to carry out some urgent repairs.

Once these repairs had been carried out, they would proceed to the assigned patrol area, having in mind their orders were now, its primary mission to carry reinforcements accomplished, to take up a patrol in the area to the north of South Georgia and carry out offensive actions against any enemy ships they located.

The small British Task Group was located, by chance, exactly there. Also, Type 22 frigate HMS *Brilliant*, commanded by Captain John Coward, was sailing at 25 knots towards the others. *Brilliant* would give the surface group a much-improved anti-submarine capability, which had only a single ASW helicopter that was equipped with a sonar, a Wessex HAS.3 (Humphrey), based on HMS *Antrim*.

At 0854 on the 25th, the *Santa Fe* was transiting north on the surface at maximum available speed in search of the safety of the deep water in which it could submerge. The sun was expected to rise at around 0930, so they would need to be submerged at 0910 at the latest. In the submarine's fin an *Teniente de Fragata* Benjamin Argañaras and two NCOs were on watch. One of the latter, Héctor "Chacho" Felman recalled:

Two Westland Lynx HAS.2 (XZ231 and XZ234) at Yeovilton, 3 September 1977. (Chris England)

Royal Navy Wasp XT417 carrying two Nord AS.12 missiles. (MoD)

A damaged ARA *Santa Fe* making for Cumberland Bay in South Georgia being engaged from several helicopters. This photograph was taken from a Lynx HAS.2 of HMS *Brilliant* (F90) while machine gunning the submarine! (Tony Smith via David Oddy)

The area was still dark, and the weather was good. I was part of the watch party. During a moment that we were in the shade of mountains in the area, I spotted something towards the stern of the submarine, at very low altitude. I focused my eyes on the object and shouted "Helicopter towards the stern! Helicopter towards the stern!"

The Officer of the Watch immediately pressed the collision alarm. The helicopter was, by now, closing from the left, and passed over to the right at about 180 metres, rapidly carried out a manoeuvre and dropped two cylinders. Reacting immediately, I shouted "Top Torpedo!" There was not an opportunity to shout again, the lapse of time between the shout and the explosion was almost instant: two depth bombs landed by the safety tank, located below the tower structure.

The *Santa Fe* had been caught on the surface by Humphrey the Wessex. Its crew (Lieutenant Commander Ian Stanley, Sub-Lieutenant Stewart Cooper, Lieutenant Chris Parry and Petty Officer Aircrewman David Fitzgerald) had been ordered to take off early, armed with two Mk 11 depth charges, in order to patrol the entrance to Cumberland Bay. The ships were some 80 nautical miles distant when they took off.

The sonar equipment had just been reinstalled in the helicopter and recalibrated, having been removed to provide more space for transport purposes, in a good demonstration of the flexibility of the Wessex helicopter and the support crew being able to adapt rapidly to changing requirements and situations.

Likewise, one of *Brilliant*'s Lynx HAS.2, XZ725, recently joined up with the *Antrim* group, had taken off at 0830 to patrol the northern coast of South Georgia. It was armed with a single Mk 46 torpedo. Finally, the Wasp helicopters of *Plymouth* and *Endurance* were on alert, armed with wire-guided AS.12 missiles. These missiles, the destructive power of their warheads equivalent to a 5-inch artillery shell, would be needed if the submarine were encountered on the surface or if any other Argentine ship tried to intervene.

Humphrey had taken off at 0810 and at 0850 it was in its patrol area; the weather was misty and the visibility extremely limited at only half a nautical mile. Having had no success in detecting anything, the observer, Lieutenant Chris Parry, made a single sweep of the area with his radar. This detected a contact, amongst the icebergs, eight miles in front of them and to the north of Banff Point.

A view from the fin of ARA *Santa Fe*. The fire team lead by "Chacho" Felman was in this spot firing at the British helicopters. (Juan Ignacio Rela)

Modern days, old camo. Now civilian-owned, Westland Wasp HAS.1 (G-KAXT) as XT787 in the markings of 829 NAS (Endurance Flight) at RNAS Culdrose in July 2013. (Chris England)

Making its way towards the contact, at three quarters of a nautical mile, they established that it was the *Santa Fe* and decided to attack immediately with both depth charges. As Lieutenant Parry recalled:

> I saw the fin of a submarine pass under the aircraft through the gap around the sonar housing and I released both depth charges…I glanced out of the starboard window. As we turned, the whole of the aft section of the submarine disappeared as two large explosions detonated either side of her casing about three-quarters of its length along and plumes of water shot up.

The depth charges exploded when the submarine was making a turn to starboard, very close to the ballast tanks. The blast from the explosion knocked out diesel engines and the submarine's electrics. However, both were soon back up and running. The biggest problem now facing the stricken submarine was that it could not safely submerge. There was damage to the diesel engines' air intake, the communications system and the hull opening indicator light panel. Likewise, the boat was now listing to starboard, which meant it was necessary to continuously blow the fuel tanks to ensure the list did not get any worse. This resulted in a great part of the submarine's fuel ending up in the sea.

In spite of all this damage, the hull of the submarine remained intact. It had, somehow, managed to survive an explosion that should have, in theory (and according to the Mk 11 mod 3 depth charge manufacturer), destroyed it. Faced with this situation, the commander of the *Santa Fe* considered it would be better to stay on the surface and

Table 8: Weapon employment against submarine ARA *Santa Fe*.

Time	Helicopter	Parent ship	Weapon	Attack results	Damage
0855	Wessex (XP142/406)	HMS *Antrim*	Mk 11 depth charges (x2)	Depth charges detonated either side of submarine hull.	Knocked out diesel engine and electrics briefly. Permanent damage to air intake valve. Submarine listing to starboard.
0902	Lynx (XZ725/341)	*HMS Brilliant*	Mk 46 torpedo	Mk 46 torpedo circled below submarine (unable to attack a surfaced target).	None
0912	Wasp (XS527/434)	HMS *Endurance*	AS.12 missile (x2)	First missile hit submarine fin and failed to explode. Second missile missed.	Severe wounds to one man and slight injuries to two others
0950	Wasp (XS527/434)	HMS *Endurance*	AS.12 missile (x2)	First missile went rogue. Second missile hit submarine fin.	Small hole in the fin
0953	Wasp (XT429/445)	HMS *Plymouth*	AS.12 missile	Missile hit the waterline of the submarine's starboard quarter.	Small dent in the hull
1010	Wasp (XS539/435)	*HMS Endurance*	AS.12 missile (x2)	First missile missed. Second missile hit submarine fin and failed to explode.	Small hole in the fin
1025	Wasp (XS527/434)	*HMS Endurance*	AS.12 missile (x2)	First missile was jettisoned. Second missile hit fin and exploded.	Larger hole in the fin

head for Grytviken as fast as possible. Once there, the troops on the ground would be able to provide some measure of anti-aircraft fire.

Another reason for not submerging was that it was thought that they would be easy prey for the nuclear-powered submarine that they considered could be in the vicinity and would have surely been alerted by the helicopter. According to the commander of *Santa Fe*: "The decision was taken to return to Grytviken, in order to save the crew. If I had ordered an immediate submersion, as required by the doctrine, we would have left an indelible datum and all the British would have to do is shoot at this target."

As the submarine made its way back towards Grytviken, the Wessex repositioned itself some distance from the submarine, firing off various bursts from its door-mounted machine gun and then hovered in order to dip its sonar (to chase the submarine in the case it submerged). At this very moment, *Capitán* Bicain had climbed up into the fin to evaluate the situation and was obliged to throw himself to the floor by the Wessex's machine gun fire. Nobody was hurt, but some damage was done to the periscope and fibreglass skin fin.

On hearing the incoming gunfire, *Cabo Principal* Héctor Felman requested permission to be allowed into the fin with a group of volunteers and reply to the fire with 7.62mm FAL and Beretta BM59 rifles – a few of which were carried by the submarine. The request was immediately authorised.

Whilst the Wessex was hovering, Lieutenant Parry, who had assumed the role of Scene of Action Commander (SAC), quickly recalled the *Brilliant*'s Lynx from its task. The Lynx, crewed by Lieutenant Commander (Lt Cdr) Barry Bryant and Lt Nick Butler, was at that moment 30 miles to the north of the *Santa Fe*. Parry also called for *Plymouth*'s Wasp helicopter to join the attack with its AS.12 missiles. The ships also increased speed and headed in the direction of the submarine.

A few minutes later, the Lynx appeared on the scene and dropped its Mk 46 torpedo close to the submarine. This weapon, through a feature of its design, would not be able to hit a vessel on the surface but, despite this, it was dropped with the aim of discouraging the *Santa Fe* from attempting to submerge. After dropping its weapon, the Lynx then climbed to about 1,000 feet (305 metres) and started to fire on the submarine with its 7.62mm machine gun and, even the pilot's 9mm pistol. Four-hundred rounds of machine gun were fired that day. The crew in the submarine's fin returned fire, forcing the Lynx to back off. However, all was not yet finished. Soon was to be the turn of the missiles.

After receiving the WOLF (brevity code for a visually identified surfaced hostile submarine) report, one of *Endurance*'s two Wasps had taken off (XS527 with Lt Cdrs Tony Ellerbeck and David Wells onboard). They found the submarine to the north of Banff Point and at 0912 fired their first missile at the submarine, after calling BRUISER LOOSE (BRUISER is the brevity word for an Air Launched Anti-Ship Missile).

According to Tony Ellerbeck:

> We were airborne in three minutes thanks to excellent work by the Greenies completing the arming circuits. As we transited north towards the place where the attack had taken place, we climbed to about 750ft and it was not long before I spotted her still heading out to sea. David was using the gyro-stabilised sight and sweeping side to side, but with no success. It took a good nudge for him to revert to a Mark 1 eyeball, but after that he was on it. We of course had no distance measuring, so guesswork came into play and David decided to hold the missile on the target rather than try to drop it in the last few hundred yards as per the textbook. We went through the pre-firing checks, selecting the starboard missile and with me saying, "your target is the submarine ahead, 3-2-1, Fire". It all started to happen. I actually called "Bruiser loose", which caused great excitement back on Mother. The missile stayed on the rail for what seemed an age and then away it went, appearing to climb until David gathered it. I had actually hit the stopwatch, but to be honest, was far more interested in watching the missile. The flare was easy to follow and David made an excellent job of guiding it home. It struck the submarine fin and passed through the fibreglass skin but hit a ladder and exploded a couple of feet beyond that.

This missile, which impacted on the rear of the submarine's fin, also removed the right leg of young *Cabo Segundo* Alberto Macías, who was there carrying ammunition to resupply the members of the crew that were firing at the British helicopters. Macías fell inside the submarine and was quickly helped by the medic. As *Suboficial Segundo* Arnaldo Funes, the submarine's NCO medic later explained:

> When they told me of the situation, I immediately went to the stern battery compartment. As I arrived there, they were bringing Macías in. He was carried to and put on one of the tables in the mess. On inspecting him, it was clear he had a traumatic wound at the right knee. He had completely lost the leg below the knee. It was important to act immediately. We injected him with some morphine that *Cabo* Milano had retrieved from the refrigerator. Also, using sterile sheets, I covered the leg and stemmed the loss of blood. To finish I put a cannula so that it would be quick and easy to administer whatever necessary medication or replace the lost blood. Once we had finished this first aid, we placed Macías on a bed in the sleeping area.

The first aid provided by *Suboficial* Funes undoubtedly save *Cabo* Macías' life. The missile impact had also caused minor injuries to two other men as well as starting a small fire, which was quickly put out.

Endurance's Wasp followed up its first missile with a second, firing from a height of 100 feet (around 30.5 metres) and three miles away. This went into the sea 20 metres (66 feet) from the submarine, and the Wasp headed back to its ship.

Around the same time, Humphrey the Wessex had headed back to its mother ship, which by now had closed to 10 miles away, in order to rearm and refuel. Also, although it was the SAC, its coordination task was very limited: it could not even talk to the *Endurance*´s Wasp, since they had non-compatible radio equipment.

During this pause, Bicain ordered his second-in-command *Capitán de Corbeta* Michelis to contact Grytviken via radio and inform them that *Santa Fe* was returning. After a few attempts, finally reported: "They are attacking me with helicopters. I have wounded men on board. I am going there."

The fight was still not over, however. After a quick rearming (and less than 40 minutes later), again Lt Cdrs Tony Ellerbeck and David Wells' Wasp had the WOLF in its sights and fired two missiles, one hitting the fin but not exploding. At 0953, *Plymouth*'s Wasp appeared on the scene. Crewed by Lt Cdr J Dransfield and Leading Aircrewman Harper, they had taken off at 0925 armed with a single AS.12 missile. The Wasp, flying at 100 feet was positioned for a beam firing at a range about 5,000 yards and, finally, after a successful flight, the missile impacted on the waterline of the submarine's starboard quarter. Without much else to do, the helicopter returned then to *Plymouth*, to rearm and refuel. The submariners felt the impact of the AS.12 and then saw a dent in the hull. However, there was no ingress of water.

After the battle. ARA *Santa Fe* partially flooded and sat on the bottom alongside a pier at South Georgia, being overflown by a Wasp HAS.1 probably from HMS *Endurance*. The submarine was re-floated in 1985, towed to deep waters and finally sunk. (MoD)

During the remaining journey of the *Santa Fe* back to Grytviken, the submarine came under more attacks by the Lynxes and Wasps.

The second of *Brilliant*'s Lynxes (XZ729, crewed by Lt Cdr John Clark and Lt Paul McKay) had taken off at 0930. It was only armed with a machine-gun, which was utilized to strafe the submarine. Lt McKay remembers:

> Our Lynx tried to keep the conning tower clear of shooters by flying strafing runs, firing the cabin mounted GPMG at the conning tower and down inside it … I climbed into the rear cabin of the Lynx to fire the gun and I remember firing several boxes of GPMG bullets of ammunition into the sail. On our last firing run the gun jammed as the barrel was overheating. Whilst John kept the Lynx in a low hover, I remember taking out my 9mm pistol and emptying that magazine into the conning tower. It was a surreal moment.

The second of *Endurance*'s Wasps arrived. This was XS539, armed with two AS.12 missiles and crewed by Lt T. Finding and aimer Leading Aircrewman R. B. Nadin. At 1010, the first of the missiles impacted the sea surface near the submarine and the other, launched at a range of less than two miles, impacted the fin but also failed to explode. *Endurance*'s Wasps were especially active during the action, firing off missiles and returning to their mother ship to rearm. The last being a hit that occurred when the submarine was already moored to the jetty in Grytviken.

At the end of the battle, *Endurance* and *Plymouth*'s Wasps had fired nine AS.12 missiles between them, of which five had hit the submarine (six launches and three hits by *Endurance*´s XS527; two launches and one hit by *Endurance*´s XS539 and one launch/one hit by Plymouth´s flight). Despite the large number of hits received from the AS.12 missiles, none of them did any serious damage or led to water ingress.

During the whole time that it was raining missiles, *Capitán* Bicain, his second-in-command *Capitán* Michelis and *Cabo* Felman, along with other members of the fire team, remained in the submarine's fin, evacuating it briefly every time a missile was about to hit. According to Felman:

> I had never seen a missile launch, but I can assure you that with two exploding nearby, you quickly become an expert. That is why every time a helicopter pointed its nose at us, we shouted "down everyone", we left the guns on the floor and we jumped from the top to the Control Room below.

Cabo Felman spent the time firing continuously and was described in HMS *Brilliant*´s diary as "one brave soul on the submarine fin" who "bravely returned machine-gun fire." Each time his rifle jammed, he would throw it overboard, into the sea, and shout down for a replacement from inside the submarine. Following the conflict, the Argentine Navy wanted to court martial Felman for the loss of the rifles, something that in the end did not take place.

Near the port at Grytviken, the fin was ordered to be cleared so that the docking manoeuvres could be carried out via the periscope. The submarine now found itself in a crossfire between the helicopters and the Argentine troops close to the jetty.

The helicopters continued to harass the *Santa Fe*, and a Bantam anti-tank missile was fired back at them from a position on the coast. From then, no more missiles were fired, and the submariners began to disembark under sporadic machine gun fire. The first to be taken off was the injured *Cabo* Macías.

It was planned to go back onboard the submarine that evening to see if it were possible to sail once again, but events overtook them. Following a demonstration of naval gunfire courtesy of HMS *Antrim* and HMS *Plymouth*, an improvised group of Royal Marines, SBS and SAS troops were landed by the very helicopters that had until very recently been shooting up the *Santa Fe*.

The Argentine marines, who had orders not to fight against superior forces, hung out white sheets on Shackleton House and the Post Office and communicated by radio at 1715 on 25 April on VHF channel 16 that they wished to surrender and that they had some wounded. For the *Santa Fe*, the war had finished.

The only fatality occurred the following day. While an attempt was being made to move the *Santa Fe* from the jetty using some Argentine crew members with British sentries, *Suboficial Primero* Felix Artuso was shot by his Royal Marine guard the moment they moved from the pier. The unfortunate Argentine was attempting to balance the listing submarine but received seven shots from the spooked guard who thought, incorrectly, that he was trying to scuttle the boat.

Both Artuso and the *Santa Fe* remain in South Georgia (Georgias del Sur) to this day. The former is buried not far from famous explorer Sir Ernest Shackleton, in Grytviken's only cemetery. After the conflict was over, the *Santa Fe* was re-floated, towed out to deeper water near the islands and sunk.

6

"DO WHALES HAVE MAGNETIC PROPERTIES?"

1 MAY

On 1 May, the tension in the British Task Force was high. Everyone was on tenterhooks. Argentine attacks were expected to occur at any moment from either the sky or from the depths of the ocean. An RAF Avro Vulcan, flying from Ascension Island, had bombed the airfield close to the capital of the islands. The time for diplomacy had finished, and hostilities had commenced over the Falklands/Malvinas.

The Task Force's sonar operators were especially busy. The actual location of the submarine ARA *Salta* was unknown. This submarine could have been anywhere, ready to fire its SST-4 torpedoes from a great distance. None of the ships wanted to be the first one sunk in the conflict that had just commenced.

The main body of the Task Force was, in the first hours of the day, some 270 nautical miles to the east of the islands. They were arranged in a formation that gave priority to the anticipated air-threat and were heading west, towards the islands.

At 0130z, the Royal Navy ships had entered the Total Exclusion Zone around the islands and the aircraft carriers were preparing their aircraft for a dawn attack on the airfields at the capital and Goose Green. The twelve Sea Harriers destined for this attack took off at 1050.

Events started unfolding at 0821. The destroyer, HMS *Sheffield*, reported a sonar contact at 30 nautical miles. This was rapidly classified as a NONSUB. *Sheffield* was ahead of the main formation providing an anti-aircraft shield, while closer to the HVUs were the frigates HMS *Brilliant* and HMS *Broadsword* on an anti-submarine screen. 820 and 826 Naval Air Squadrons were at maximum effort, providing three Sea Kings each for the anti-submarine protection task ("Ripple 3") as well as an additional one to carry out a surface search for naval targets.

Half an hour after *Sheffield*'s first alert, another contact was investigated – which turned out to be a whale. HMS *Brilliant* detected another contact at just two miles, which it classified as POSSUB LOW 1, later increasing the classification to POSSUB LOW 2. The frigate felt that it had a solid sonar contact and therefore left the anti-submarine screen to pursue it. After manoeuvring into a position to engage this contact, *Brilliant* launched two Mk 46 anti-submarine torpedoes from its deck launchers (at 1003 and 1009). These both exploded not long after entering the sea. The ship's commander, Captain John Coward, was absolutely convinced that he was attacking an enemy submarine. He ordered one of the ship's Lynxes into the air to carry out an extensive search with its MAD (Magnetic Anomaly Detector) equipment. They found nothing.

One of the MAD equipped Lynx HAS.2 of HMS *Broadsword* was also tasked to investigate (being airborne since 0949), and the Flight Commander, Lieutenant Commander Rick Jones later reported: "347 was launched twice with Skuas loaded to see if whales had any magnetic properties. Dolphins seem more interesting, as they show up as a 'sinker' as well as a sonar contact. Later in the day a cloud was investigated for hostile intent."

During these few hours, waves, whales and even floating seaweed had been confused for a submarine. Possibly, it was a whale that was attacked by *Brilliant*. This idea was strengthened when some whale oil was spotted on the surface. Either one or both torpedoes fired must have hit the unfortunate sea mammal. At 1040, the elusive contact was finally classified as NONSUB.

Shortly after this incident, *Brilliant* and *Yarmouth* detached from the Task Force in order to carry out offensive operations against the *San Luis* – something we shall look at in more detail later.

At 1245, after a period of calm in the anti-submarine operations, but a period of intense anti-aircraft activity, the nerves again focused under the sea. The sensors of the frigates HMS *Alacrity* and HMS *Arrow* picked up the unmistakeable sound of a heavy torpedo. All the ships nearby went to Action Stations and conducted torpedo

A Sea King HAS.2 (right) and another Sea King HAS.5 at RNAS Culdrose, September 1981. (Chris England)

countermeasures, manoeuvring violently to evade.

HMS *Plymouth*, which was some ten nautical miles away from the other two frigates, corroborated the contact a short time later and concluded that there was a submarine nearby: "Positive identification." Two ASW Sea Kings flew over to assist the *Plymouth*, which had started at 1300 to use its Limbo mortar to fire a salvo. The sea was seething from the explosions from the mortars when a lookout on the aircraft carrier HMS *Invincible* reported that he had spotted a submarine periscope at scarcely 2,000 yards from the carrier.

Type 209 submarine ARA *Salta*'s masts. From left to right: attack periscope, snorkel and ESM mast. (Armada Argentina)

One of the Sea Kings turned around and dropped an anti-submarine torpedo on the target which, at that moment, had been classified as a POSSUB HIGH 4. However, the contact could not be regained. Eyes and sensors were nervously scanning the sea. Once again, the abundant sea life of the South Atlantic was making the Royal Navy suffer. The contact was later reclassified as NONSUB and the heavy torpedo that had been detected earlier could have been one of the fleet's towed decoys. The commander of *Plymouth* later reflected that:

> *Plymouth* fought a hectic ASW action between 1300 – 1400 with Dippers (Sea King equipped with dipping sonar) and a MAD Lynx, and I was at one stage convinced that we had forced the Argentinian submarine *Salta* to the surface, only to be informed by the bridge that the black object surfacing close to the ships was, after all, a school of whales! Sonar 162 produced a most convincing trace, torpedo Hydrophone Effect (HE) had been detected by two or three units, and a periscope had even been sighted by another. The abundance of marine life was to inflict further spurious delaying contacts on the Task Group throughout the day.

The day produced various other dramatic submarine alerts, all of which were discarded as NONSUB once investigated. *Arrow*, *Alacrity* and *Glamorgan* had several scares that afternoon, *Arrow* even informing via radio about a WOLF at 1704. Ian Inskip, HMS Glamorgan´s navigation officer, recalled:

> At 1704, a possible submarine was reported on the surface. It was on the bearing of Cape Pembroke Light and I suggested that it was the lighthouse. The contact was then reported as a possible conning tower with smoke. I once again reported to the ops room that there was also smoke on the bearing coming from fires ashore and that the reported contact was Cape Pembroke. It was not until 1748 that I convinced everyone.

Curiously, this contact was investigated and discarded by a Wessex HU.5 helicopter (Yankee Tango) armed with AS.12 missiles.

The last of the day's events at the core of the fleet occurred when at 1857 HMS *Glamorgan* spotted a periscope at a distance of two nautical miles – a contact that was also picked up by the sonar. So, a

HMS *Arrow* (F173) in a 1982 exercise with the US Navy. (US Navy)

torpedo in a snake search pattern was launched three minutes later from *Glamorgan's* STWS. According to Inskip, the torpedo was not fired in the end, but the official report says otherwise. An ASW helicopter was sent over to the datum and, after lowering its sonar, it was concluded that this mysterious object was nothing more than a semi-submerged rock.

At the time, *Glamorgan*, along with *Alacrity* and *Arrow* had left the vicinity of the Task Force as they had been tasked with a mission to bombard the airfield near the island's capital. They detached at 1120 and set course to the south east. Therefore, these last contacts were detected in a position very close to the islands.

The main body of the fleet had a day full of submarine alerts, but only the whales and maybe some dolphins suffered the wrath of the British torpedoes and Limbo mortars.

The commander of HMS *Arrow* (Commander Paul Bootherstone) reflected after the war: "Sonar operators need more submarine contact time for training and more emphasis needs to be placed on classification of contacts."

The real action began a couple of hours later, north of the islands.

7
"GO FIND HIM AND BRING ME BACK HIS HAT"

THE *SAN LUIS*: 1 MAY

During the evening hours of 27 April, an intelligence report received by the Task Force and the FOSM (Flag Officer Submarines) indicated that submarine ARA *San Luis* would be heading to area MARIA, to the north of the islands. The Argentine submarine patrol areas, named ironically after famous British royal women, had been known by the British for several days.

This information had probably been supplied by CGHQ (Government Communications Headquarters), located in the suburbs of Cheltenham. They had managed to break the Argentine cipher keys with the help of the Unites States NSA (National Security Agency). The Crypto encipher machines that belonged to the Argentine Navy were not at all secure. The communications might have been captured by a listening station in Ascension, New Zealand, Chile, by the US Embassy in Buenos Aires (according to rumours) or even by a communications interception satellite called Vortex (the third in the series). The NRO (National Reconnaissance Office) of the United States later admitted that the satellite, launched in October 1981, was used to support the British during the conflict. At the time, the satellite was positioned to intercept communications in Central America, but for several hours each day, the aerials were reoriented to cover the South Atlantic to gather Argentine military radio traffic and with British personnel in control of it.

With this information, FOSM (Vice-Admiral Sir Peter Herbert) ordered the nuclear hunter-killer HMS *Spartan* to set up a patrol line north of the Falklands/Malvinas. The idea was to intercept the Argentine submarine before it reached the area MARIA. The depth there was insufficient for a nuclear submarine to operate safely. After a fast transit, very early the next day (28 April) the British submarine was positioned to find and destroy *San Luis*. According to its CO (Commander James Taylor): "Established ASW patrol in area PIG 3 SIERRA, searching along likely enemy track with finger on the trigger. Sonar sea state is 4, which whilst giving cover for my increased radiated noise, has reduced likely initial detection range…No contact."

In fact, in his Report of Proceedings, Commander Taylor reflected the sonar detection range was very low for a Type 209 on main motors, especially considering that the *Spartan* lacked a towed array sonar:

> The attempted intercept of a Type 209 submarine was hampered by high biologics despite purposely clearing the Falkland Islands shelf. The search was conducted downslope to exclude the heaviest… biological noise from the threat axis but sonar sea states remained above four and predicted detection ranges were less than one thousand yards.

The chances of an encounter were slim. And, in fact, the Argentine submarine passed near the *Spartan* around noon. Both sonar teams unaware the enemy boat was nearby, even when *San Luis* was snorkelling from 1235 to 1410. The Argentine submarine cancelled the manoeuvre when its ESM equipment caught an X-band radar racket.

The next day, the *Spartan* continued its patrol, also sighting two fishing vessels and a factory ship (probably from the Soviet bloc). But soon it was re-tasked to deal with the Argentine Carrier Battle Group and abandoned the fruitless search of the *San Luis*.

A view of the bow of HMS *Brilliant* (F90) and, behind, another Type 22 frigate, possibly HMS *Battleaxe* (F89) during Exercise SPRINGTRAIN 82, shortly before April 1982. (via David Oddy)

Smile for the camera! *Cabo Primero* José Claudio Tureo (left) sitting in front of the (then broken) VM8/24 Fire Control Computer and *Cabo Primero* Oscar Alberto Serrano in front of the Atlas AN-525 A6 passive sonar console. (via Fernando Azcueta)

1 May 1982. The hunter and the hunted. ARA *San Luis* launching an SST-4 torpedo against a surface target (1305z) and being attacked with an aerial torpedo (1500z), probably a Mk 46. Neither torpedo hit its target. (artists impressions by Andrea Assanelli)

Now closer to the islands on 1 May, the commander of Carrier Battle Group, Rear Admiral Woodward, from his HQ aboard the aircraft carrier HMS *Hermes*, ordered the frigates *Brilliant* and *Yarmouth* (Commander Tony Morton) to detach themselves from the main body of the Group and head to MARIA. The mission of this search attack unit (SAU): to hunt and sink the Argentine submarine. *Brilliant*'s commander, Captain John Coward, recalled:

> One night *Brilliant* went chasing submarines, which proved rather less than successful. I had received a typical Woodward signal: 'An aircraft has reported sighting a submarine twenty miles north of Port Stanley. Go find him and bring me back his hat.'

At 1200z, the two ships broke off and by 1205z they were in an anti-submarine formation on a bearing of 260° at 24 knots and 2,000 yards apart. Every now and again, the formation changed, or they slowed down temporarily to improve the reception conditions of their sonar in a technique called sprint and drift.

Three ASW Sea Kings of 826 NAS from *Hermes* were also assigned to support the ships and their three embarked helicopters, the first of which reported to *Brilliant* at 1545z. The search had started in earnest shortly before. The Sea Kings were under the command of Lt Cdr A.J.M. Hogg (who had received the Air Force Cross for his part in the rescue of the trawler *Ben Aslade* in December 1978) and, foreseeing a long day ahead, each of the Sea Kings carried an entire spare crew of four on board. These crews were disembarked on the warships to await their shifts.

The helicopters returned periodically to the frigates in order to refuel. As they were too large to land safely on these two ships, the Cabs were refuelled by hovering over the ship's stern and pulling up a fuel line. The whole operation took fifteen minutes, and they then returned to their tasks. Sea King HAS.5 XZ577 achieved this day a record operational sortie, because the helicopter remained airborne for 10 hours and 20 minutes.

Brilliant reported arriving at area MARIA at 1700z, and signalled:

> WE ARE PROBABLY ABOUT 20-25 MILES NORTH OF MCBRIDE´S HEAD AND IN THE AREA WE ARE LIKELY TO FIND *SAN LUIS*

A post war (circa 1983) photograph of an 820 NAS Sea King HAS.5 in an ASW exercise, carrying out a weapon drop. (Steve George)

Even before the British ships were tasked with finding the *San Luis*, it had already had a few scares that day. *San Luis* had started the day moving at a low speed near the centre of MARIA. For some hours it had been heading stealthily, with no masts breaking the surface and no radio traffic, in an east-south-east direction. At 1055, *Teniente de Fragata* Alejando Maegli was on watch on the bridge when the sonar operator announced: "Sir, I have a contact". The *Teniente* called for the Captain, and he ordered him to: "Wake everyone up and get them to go to their action stations". Maegli obeyed the order:

> Azcueta warned me not to call the crew on the tannoy, as it would generate unwanted noise. I had to go to the bunks and wake them up, one by one. I remember the faces. We are all ready to be called, but when one says to you, "Take on the emergency air breather … the adrenaline started to circulate"

The contact was distant, on a bearing of 079 and was classified as a helicopter. A little later, on a similar bearing, they started to pick up active sonar emissions of 6 and 8 kHz. The tension was rising inside the *San Luis*. At 1240 another contact appeared, and the sonar team began to track it. Later, when analysing the contact's audio signature, it was classified as being either a Type 21 or 22 frigate. The ship was using its Type 184 sonar, which was well known by the Argentine Navy: this same system was fitted to their two Type 42 destroyers, ARA *Hércules* and ARA *Santísima Trinidad*, sister ships of HMS *Sheffield*. The enemy contact speed was estimated at around 18 knots. Also, from various other bearings, sonar emissions of 5, 6, 7, 8 and 10.5 kHz were detected.

*Teniente de Corbet*a Luis Seghezzi, the young pilot of the *San Luis*, left his post at eleven o´clock and went to bed, but he was rudely awakened shortly after, when "action stations" were ordered:

> We had multiple contacts, with emissions of active sonars. We were finally in front of the British fleet! What started as a remote possibility was already a certainty. In the blink of an eye, I found myself connected to the monitoring circuit that was being coordinated by the Executive Officer. That, along with other stations, fulfilled the function of filtering and refining data regarding the estimated distance from potential targets. The Commander remained alert, observing, evaluating, moving from one station to another. The activity in the Control Room resembled a scene from a movie. I was working on the charts, but I could not stop thinking about how unreal everything seemed to me. At one point I turned a little, and I noticed a young *Cabo Segundo* who did not have an assigned combat role. He had come as close as he could to the Control Room to try to observe and understand what was happening. When I looked him in the eyes, I think his face reflected the expression I had on my own face – one of stupor.

Capitán de Fragata Azcueta ordered the submarine to close on the target, temporarily increasing speed. When he felt that he should be able to spot it, he exposed the attack periscope for a few seconds. However, he could not see anything due to a haze that blurred the vision through the scope. What was certain was that the submarine's periscope was not detected while out of the water. As the submarine commander explained:

> I only exposed the periscope once, and for a short period of time during the approach to the target. I had one look, but I was unable to see anything. I was very conservative in the use of the periscope as the surface of the sea was like a lake (Sea State 0), the worst type of surface for exposing any kind of mast. I did not see the target, but because the high rate of change in the contact bearing (three degrees per minute), I concluded that we were easily within torpedo range of it. I did not use the active sonar, as it would have given away my position.

At 1305, estimating that the target would be at around 9,500 yards, Maegli informed Azcueta: "Sir, the fire solution is ready". At this moment, the submarine was at a depth of 30 metres (around 98 feet) and on a bearing of 140°, target angle was 015° and the angle on the bow was port 20°. Azcueta ordered an SST-4 torpedo to be fired manually and in emergency mode. This was the only possibility because, as previously mentioned, the Fire Control Computer was still broken.

"Fire!" The torpedo was fired from tube number four at an initially slow speed-setting in passive mode (in order not to reveal its presence to the target), and on a snake search pattern. The torpedo's course was set to 004°.

Azcueta later wrote in the submarine's war diary about the reason for shooting from such a distance.

> I decided to shoot from a long distance in consideration that during the run of the torpedo the distance to the target would reduce considerably as the submarine and target were heading towards each other. Also, the proximity of a helicopter might mean that we would need to begin evasive manoeuvres at any moment.

In order to facilitate the steering of the torpedo, the commander ordered the submarine to stop (the *San Luis* had been moving at 4 knots). As the torpedo sped away from the submarine, inside there was total silence. According to *Teniente de Corbeta* Seghezzi:

> For a moment, I stopped paying attention to my work and focused on what was about to happen. From a deep tone that was increasing in intensity, the torpedo propellers began to beat the water confined in the small space of the launch tube. A fast-paced vibration was amplified, and it quickly spread throughout the submarine. It was a few seconds, until the torpedo moved free of the guides and abandoned its confinement, running free.

ARA *San Luis´* planesman, *Cabo Principal* Alberto Poskin sleeps at his combat station during a pause in the action. (via Daniel Mesa)

Capitán de Navío Eulogio Moya Latrubesse (Argentine Submarine Force Commanding Officer) talking with *Capitán de Fragata* Fernando Azcueta (*San Luis´* Commanding Officer) moments after the submarine arrived back at Puerto Belgrano Naval Base. In between the men is *Cabo Primero* Damian Washington "Piti" Riveros. (via Fernando Azcueta)

After two minutes, Azcueta, realising that the target had moved, ordered a small correction in the trajectory of the torpedo. The torpedo received the order, but seconds later the submarine's control computer displayed the "wire cut" error. The sonar team quickly corroborated this. They heard a knock on the hull consistent with a physical breaking of the guidance wire between the torpedo and the submarine and so it was not a case of an electronic problem. The torpedo was no longer connected to the submarine.

However, this did not mean that the torpedo was now lost. From the moment the wire connection to it was gone the torpedo would, in theory, continue on its programmed run. Once the torpedo arrived at its destination, it would then begin to use its own sonar for its attack, as explained by *Teniente de Navío* Alessandrini:

> The torpedo has a sonar fitted in its head. Therefore, if the guidance wire is cut, this does not necessarily mean that the torpedo is lost. If the calculations have been made correctly, the torpedo would continue its course towards the target. However, there could have been a thousand and one other factors for the failure. What is true was that an explosion was not heard in the submarine.

This was clear after they had waited 44 minutes, the maximum endurance of the torpedo fired: no explosion was heard. The problem of losing the guidance wire for the torpedoes was something that

Westland Lynx HAS.2 XZ729 (342) refuelling on HMS *Brilliant*. (via David Oddy)

plagued the *San Luis* throughout the conflict, in the same way the *Salta* had suffered in its test firings. Post-war studies concluded that:

> The torpedo should leave the tube with a predetermined run depth equal to or greater than the depth of the keel of the submarine. If it was fired with a shallower depth programmed than the submarine was at, it was certain that the submarine would run over the wire, causing it to break. However, in the case of firing the torpedoes using the emergency mode, as carried out by the *San Luis*, the torpedo would automatically travel through the water at a depth of 12 feet (3.6 metres), its depth could not be programmed otherwise. Therefore, each time one was fired using this mode, it would run for a few minutes and the wire would be cut by the submarine.

Nobody in the Argentine Navy was aware of this vital snippet of information. Equally, as previously stated, the torpedoes were not exactly in tiptop condition. It remains a mystery which ship the *San Luis* fired its torpedo at. There were no British ships in the vicinity, and nor was it detected by any of the ships hunting the *San Luis*. It is entirely possible that the target the *San Luis* fired at was at a much greater distance than was estimated, especially considering that the DUUX equipment, a passive sonar utilised to measure target distances, had been suffering from reliability problems.

Azcueta later noted in the war diary that "I have appreciated that due to the good propagation of sound through the water, the contact must have been further away than thought". The commander of submarine HMS *Splendid*, Roger Lane-Nott, made a very similar entry in his diary on 4 May: "sonar ranges are exceptionally good and tends to confirm that we have been severely under-ranging for the past 24 hours".

Shortly after this disappointment, Azcueta ordered a course change towards the south west at slow speed. By now, the noises being picked up by the submarine's sonar were becoming stronger and the sound of helicopters dipping their sonar in the sea were being clearly detected. The contact that had been fired at had also been lost, the sound being masked out by the noise made by their own torpedo on its long run.

At 1500z, in a tense atmosphere with helicopters in the air, pings from active sonars being heard, one or more British frigates out there and the thought that *San Luis* had revealed its presence by launching the torpedo, the sonar operator *Suboficial Segundo* Ernesto Errecalde shouted words nobody onboard the submarine wanted to hear: "Torpedo splash in the water!"

Azcueta immediately ordered "All ahead full", with which the submarine began to cavitate. This was not good, because cavitation – a noise generated by bubbles collapsing – could be heard at a considerable distance by any passive sonar. But speed in a submarine sometimes comes at a price. At the same time, he ordered FLB countermeasures to be deployed and *Cabo Principal* González launched two noise-making decoys at once. These devices, which produced bubbles in order to distract and confuse torpedoes, were commonly referred as Alka-Stelzers, after the effervescent antacid, in the Argentine Navy. The *San Luis* was carrying a stock of 24 of these devices.

A short time later, the commander ordered the motors to stop, and to gain depth while in a port turn. The idea behind this manoeuvre was that the torpedo be seduced by the countermeasures, while the submarine "disappeared" from the sonar search cone of the enemy weapon. As no "pings" were detected, it was assumed that the torpedo was using only its passive sonar. Just as that move was complete, the sonar operator announced: "torpedo closing on the stern". And all hearts inside the boat skipped a beat.

By now all those onboard the submarine could hear the throb of the torpedo´s propeller through the hull of the submarine. "It sounded a little like a motorcycle engine, but under the water" recalled *Teniente de Fragata* Jorge Fernando Dacharry, the head of Electrics.

Everyone thought that the torpedo was about to hit them. *Cabo Principal* Alberto Fernando Poskin, one of the submarine's planesmen, recalled that moment:

> For a few seconds, I experienced the joy of fear. It was a sensation I had experienced several times before, but this time it felt like it was going to be the last time. I would like to say that it was the best and most memorable of all my fears. It was as if my soul had relaxed, it had a different attitude and it was being carried by the moment. The final moment of destiny.

Ten seconds later, the sonarman Errecalde who was a couple of metres from *Cabo* Poskin, announced that the torpedo had passed over the other side. There was a huge sigh of relief. From then, almost constant explosions were heard. The submarine changed course various times, but the sonar operators were still picking up the sounds of nearby ships. According to *Teniente de Corbeta* Seghezzi:

> From that moment, the Commander focused on all the necessary manoeuvres to carry out an evasion that would allow us to leave

the focus of attention. The idea was to try to have a chance again to attack some other target. But the reality was that the submarine was constantly manoeuvring to evade the entire time, changing course and depth in a relentless replay.

Azcueta, feeling somewhat harassed and with few options remaining, decided to settle the submarine on the seabed at 1925. They were in shallow water, under 50 metres (164 feet), and a few miles off McBride Head (Península de San Luis). *Cabo* Poskin recalled:

> One moment, the commander ordered the motors stopped and to settle onto the seabed. When the speed dropped off, to approximately six knots, the bow made contact with the bottom but then started to rise again. Fortunately, at that moment, a member of the crew – *Cabo Primero* Damian Washington Riveros (affectionately known as "Piti") – without having received any order, at that precise moment opened one of the compensator valves on the torpedo tank on the bow and flooded it. This action made the bow of the submarine heavy, which resulted in it bouncing four or five times on the seabed, but prevented any damage occurring to the submarine's propeller or rudders by their digging into the seabed. If this had happened, we might never have left the bottom.

The submarine remained on the bottom until 0005 on 2 May. To save oxygen, and so the crew could get some rest, Azcueta ordered that they leave their action stations and go to their bunks.

Explosions continued around *San Luis*. The commander knew that many of these explosions would be depth charges or mortar salvoes, but others were felt as low-powered explosions that were launched as a deterrent. "They did deter us", *Capitán* Azcueta philosophised after the war. However, *Brilliant*, *Yarmouth* and the three 826 NAS helicopters were not at all close to the *San Luis*, but some miles to the north.

During this day, these ships would have two remarkable incidents. One of them started at 1811, when HMS *Yarmouth* attacked a submerged contact with four salvoes of its Limbo mortar. The target had been confirmed by the MAD fitted to one of the Sea Kings. Moments later, the Sea King thought that a periscope had been seen in this location, though the many birds in the area created doubt about the sighting, and dropped a depth charge on it. *Yarmouth*'s Wasp also helped in the attack.

Sub Lieutenant Paul Freemantle was the Observer on board one of the Sea Kings, the rest of the crew were made up of Lt Cdr Hogg – also 826's senior pilot, Sub Lieutenant Steve Gibson and an Aircrewman, which was taking part in the hunt for the *San Luis*. He recalled:

> A contact was detected on active sonar which was attacked with torpedoes and depth charges. My aircraft was fitted with Magnetic Anomaly Detector (MAD) and, as myself and my crewman had been members of the MAD trials team, I decided to stream the bird. We detected a solid contact in the vicinity of the sonar contact. We then instructed *Yarmouth*'s Wasp, which was carrying two depth charges, to fly in formation with the MAD bird and drop on my command. We did detect an oil slick on the sea surface but this likely to be from the depth charges.

The hunt ceased abruptly at 1915 due to an Air Raid Warning Red. At 1935, having had the all clear from the air raid alert, both ships returned to hunt for the elusive submarine. They located a promising contact to the north of MARIA and having had, again, a firm MAD contact, at 2010 *Brilliant* fired a Mk 44 and another Mk 46 in its direction. On top of this, *Yarmouth* carried out another Limbo mortar attack, and further depth charges were dropped by Sea King at 2130. This contact was later classified as a wreck.

Up on the surface, Brilliant's commander, John Coward, was faced with a problem – they did not have enough bombs to cover each bottomed contact. One of them was probably the elusive Argentine submarine. And the area was full of old wrecks.

At 2345, after these two main incidents and dozens of other scares, the ships were ordered to re-join the Task Force. The helicopters belonging to 826 NAS had returned a little before. *Brilliant*'s CO later recorded this day in his diary:

> I knew if we found him, he'd be on the bottom and the whole place was littered with old whaling ships. We would find something, ping on it and it would look about the size of a small submarine, so we'd fly a helicopter with a magnetic detector over it and, yes, it would say it's metal. But I didn't have enough bombs to cover each wreck, and very few helicopters with metal detectors on them. The place was also full of whales, which gave enormous echoes on the sonar. Every so often a whale would come up, give a little blow, and a flock of seagulls would gather round, appearing as a quick flash on the radar. Everybody would say, 'Christ, it must be a submarine,' and we launched a few torpedoes at things like that. All in all, it was a total frustration but, looking back, I've a feeling that one of those wrecks was the *San Luis* and I think that eventually the analysis boys will confirm it.

However, none of the wrecks attacked that day were the *San Luis*; it was still hiding to the south of the zone being searched by the frigates. Lieutenant Commander Barry Bryant, *Brilliant*'s flight commander gave a slightly different point of view of 1 May 1982 in his operational report: "A day remembered for numerous attacks on non-subs, an influx of firm sonar and MAD contacts and the day the whales of the Southern Ocean began their journey north, minus a few of their numbers."

The day did not end there for HMS *Yarmouth*. At 0200, while returning to the Carrier Group, the *Yarmouth* gained a contact at just two miles, which at the time was considered to be the best contact they had had all day. At 0235, they attacked it with a salvo from the Limbo mortar. It was later classified as NONSUB. The contact was a long way from the *San Luis*'s location, which by now was travelling in an east-south-east direction outside area MARIA.

At 0245, the *San Luis* picked up what was the last contact of the day, which it considered to be helicopters to the south of its position. There were also sonar emissions coming from the south, which the commander thought were surface ships, and as well to the north. However, the latter were somewhat weak and distant. He ordered the crew to action-stations once again and started to approach the contacts to the south. Shortly after turning towards the contact, they decided that the only way that they would be able to reach them would be with a high-speed run. However, the battery level was now 73%, and the level of carbon dioxide in the submarine's atmosphere was now at a dangerous level of 2%. Therefore, the decision was taken by *Capitán* Azcueta not to pursue these contacts because of: "an exhausted crew due to the harassment and events of the previous day". The day was over.

The submarine went back to sit on the sea floor and continued to detect sonar emissions. At 0815 of 2 May, it raised its snorkel and other masts in order to charge the batteries, circulate some fresh air through the submarine and send a report about its operations of the previous day.

Inside the *San Luis*, *Cabo Primero Enfermero* Rafael Guaraz recorded the following in his personal diary:

> I think that the 1 May will forever be present in my mind, and in those of all who are onboard, as the longest, agonising, unhappy and desperate day of our lives until now. Until now, I have never felt so close to the end as I did yesterday. The hunt continued the whole of the day and on into the early hours of today (2 May). We were very close to the coast and we were hoping that the aircraft on the Malvinas would help us, but we did not realise that they were also fighting fiercely – even though we did think that this might be the case. When we snorkelled, we found out what had been going on as we could listen to the news on the radio.

The question remains as to who launched the torpedo that almost hit the *San Luis*? At the time (1500z), the 826 NAS Sea Kings were still en route to MARIA, the two frigates were far from the submarine's recorded position and the *Yarmouth´s* Wasp had no capabilities to prosecute and engage a submerged target. The likely candidates are either *Brilliant´s* Lynx HAS.2 or, more probably, XZ729 crewed by Lt Cdr John Clark and Lt Paul McKay. According to Paul McKay:

> This was during my first sortie which started with a coastal reconnaissance before the ASW action started in earnest. We dropped a Mk 46 torpedo in this sortie.
>
> Today I am still confident the torpedo I dropped on her was one which came very close. Those 6 minutes and after we scanned the surface expecting to see signs of oil etc .... we did see oil that day on other engagements but could have been whale or wreck detritus.
>
> Starting the day high on expectation and as history tells surviving a *San Luis* torpedo attack, night fell and we thought we had given *San Luis* a run for her money. Credit to the fighting and tactical skill of the submarine to evade the very best of ASW forces thrown at prosecuting her. I am happy today that the outcome to Argentine and British ASW players was a nil sum game. It was a close-run battle of minds and nerves. Well done to *San Luis* for her cunning that day. Sorry for the whales and wrecks which took a beating though!

8

"POSSIBLY IT WAS A SUBMARINE FROM ANOTHER NAVY"

5 MAY AND 11 MAY

ACT ONE

Aircraft carrier HMS *Invincible*. Torpedoes from the flight deck

On 5 May, HMS *Invincible* was in the main body of the Task Force with its close escort ship, HMS *Brilliant*, alongside her. According to the ship´s war diary, it was: "a quiet day with the depressing and gloomy weather, consisting of low cloud, poor visibility and rain, matching the sombre mood on board as the full impact of yesterday´s event sinks in".

Morale had been affected by the events of the previous day: HMS *Sheffield* had been hit by an Exocet, and a Sea Harrier had been shot down during an attack on Goose Green. Before sunrise, the Carrier Group had had several submarine alerts, but they all had been quickly classified as false alarms. However, at 1156z, *Brilliant*'s sonar operators detected what they thought to be a torpedo. This detection was rapidly confirmed via the Type 184 sonar fitted to *Invincible*. At around the same time, two of the ship's flight-deck crew reported seeing the wake of a torpedo to the starboard of the ship. According to Petty Officer Rod Fearnley:

> I was near the round down at the time, when we saw it, with one of my killicks, L/A McLean…I saw and reported what I thought was a cavitation trail coming from our Port quarter. It seemed odd that just before I saw it, Vince [*Invincible*] up skirted and went to flank speed.

A Sea King HAS.5 of 820 NAS flying over the islands shortly after the Argentine surrender. (Steve George)

On sounding the alert, the carrier began to make high-speed evasion manoeuvres and the crew were ordered to brace for the impact of a torpedo. For many of the crew, this was the worst moment of the conflict, worse than even the various Exocet attacks that took place on the fleet.

Invincible's sonar operator at the time recalls the event:

> The HE (Hydrophone Effect) operator anyway he pipes up what the fucks

this, the HE display has a huge orange spike at green 30, I switch into the HE and had a listen, it was a very fast propeller and loud, I swivelled around to look at the radar display, switched to air, could be a helo hovering, nope, switched to surface, could be a small fast boat, nothing.

It was at this point that I decided that I knew what it was, I think I knew anyway but I was scared of making a fool of myself, if that makes sense!

I leaned over and pressed the torpedo alarm, "green 30 torpedo torpedo torpedo green 30 centre bearing 270" the alarm was repeated on the bridge and within seconds the OOW (Officer of the Watch) went through his procedure, the ship sped up and turned towards the contact. We continued to track the HE and it was running straight at us (no gyro problems with this one!) I asked for permission to go active, which was given, and almost immediately we got a contact at about 10,000 yards on the same bearing as the HE, which I classified as a submarine, at the same time we tracked the HE coming straight towards us and then down our starboard side, we then turned 180° and went to full power. We lost contact with the submarine when it went into our stern wash.

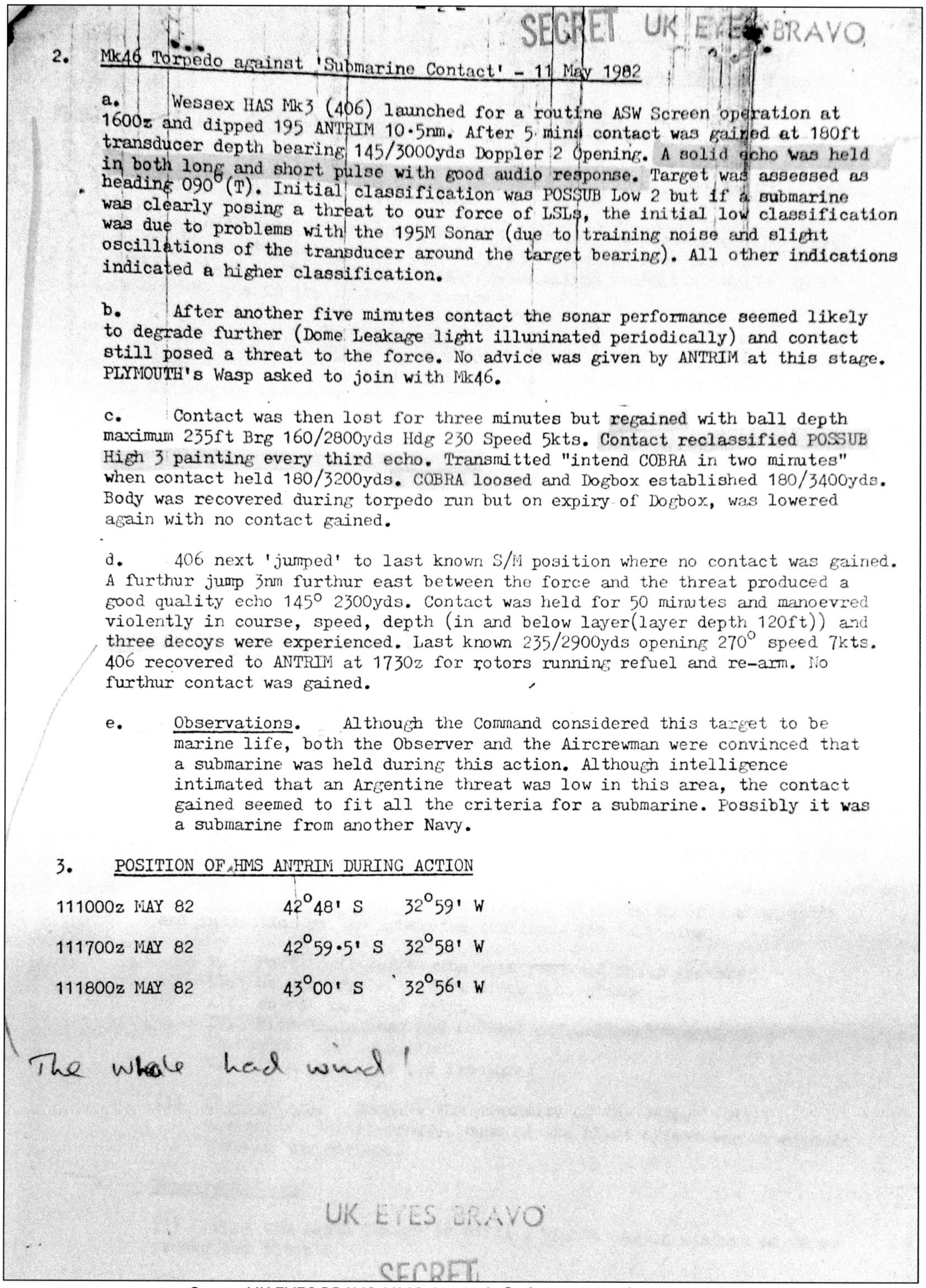

SECRET UK EYES BRAVO

2. Mk46 Torpedo against 'Submarine Contact' – 11 May 1982

a. Wessex HAS Mk3 (406) launched for a routine ASW Screen operation at 1600z and dipped 195 ANTRIM 10·5nm. After 5 mins contact was gained at 180ft transducer depth bearing 145/3000yds Doppler 2 Opening. A solid echo was held in both long and short pulse with good audio response. Target was assessed as heading 090° (T). Initial classification was POSSUB Low 2 but if a submarine was clearly posing a threat to our force of LSLs, the initial low classification was due to problems with the 195M Sonar (due to training noise and slight oscillations of the transducer around the target bearing). All other indications indicated a higher classification.

b. After another five minutes contact the sonar performance seemed likely to degrade further (Dome Leakage light illuninated periodically) and contact still posed a threat to the force. No advice was given by ANTRIM at this stage. PLYMOUTH's Wasp asked to join with Mk46.

c. Contact was then lost for three minutes but regained with ball depth maximum 235ft Brg 160/2800yds Hdg 230 Speed 5kts. Contact reclassified POSSUB High 3 painting every third echo. Transmitted "intend COBRA in two minutes" when contact held 180/3200yds. COBRA loosed and Dogbox established 180/3400yds. Body was recovered during torpedo run but on expiry of Dogbox, was lowered again with no contact gained.

d. 406 next 'jumped' to last known S/M position where no contact was gained. A furthur jump 3nm furthur east between the force and the threat produced a good quality echo 145° 2300yds. Contact was held for 50 minutes and manoevred violently in course, speed, depth (in and below layer(layer depth 120ft)) and three decoys were experienced. Last known 235/2900yds opening 270° speed 7kts. 406 recovered to ANTRIM at 1730z for rotors running refuel and re-arm. No furthur contact was gained.

e. Observations. Although the Command considered this target to be marine life, both the Observer and the Aircrewman were convinced that a submarine was held during this action. Although intelligence intimated that an Argentine threat was low in this area, the contact gained seemed to fit all the criteria for a submarine. Possibly it was a submarine from another Navy.

3. POSITION OF HMS ANTRIM DURING ACTION

111000z MAY 82 42°48' S 32°59' W

111700z MAY 82 42°59·5' S 32°58' W

111800z MAY 82 43°00' S 32°56' W

The whale had wind!

UK EYES BRAVO

SECRET

Secret UK EYES BRAVO HMS *Antrim's* flight report: Mk 46 Torpedo against "Submarine Contact" – 11 May 1982. (MoD)

The aircraft carrier headed to the north-west at high speed while *Brilliant* went to investigate the contact, joined by two Sea Kings from 826 NAS. They did not find anything.

A post-war analysis determined that it would be very difficult for the sonar fitted to the aircraft carrier to detect an Argentine torpedo. It also concluded that this type of electric torpedo would not leave a wake of bubbles which could be spotted on the surface. It was concluded that no attack had taken place and that the contacts had been spurious. "Not everyone is convinced" recorded *Invincible*'s war diary, as a mark of non-conformity with this conclusion.

Given the immense gravity of the incident, the crew of the aircraft carrier were instructed not to discuss it, and neither was it recorded in the fleet diary of the conflict. However, somewhat surprisingly, the next day the news of the scare appeared in at least one national newspaper in the UK.

A year after the conflict, a story appeared in the press that the commander of the *San Luis* had shadowed the aircraft carrier for six days before launching four torpedoes at it, all of them hitting the ship below the waterline without exploding.

This story was entirely fictional. Azcueta had never claimed this. In fact, on that day, the *San Luis* was still in an area to the north of McBride Head (Península de San Luis), a long way from where the *Invincible* and its escorts were operating. It is also worth recalling that the *Santa Fe* was no longer in Argentine hands and the *Salta* was still in port. So, if there had been a submarine and torpedo that day, neither could possibly have been Argentine.

ACT TWO

Wessex HAS.3: POSSUB 4

At 1600 on 11 May, Humphrey, the Wessex HAS.3 based on HMS *Antrim* which had already successfully detected and damaged the ARA *Santa Fe* in South Georgia, was airborne on ASW duties in the protection of a small convoy of logistics ships including the RFA landing ships and the tankers *Pearleaf* and *Plumleaf*. HMS *Plymouth* was the other escort for the convoy, and its Wasp HAS.1 helicopter was on deck on an eight-minute alert, armed with a single Mk 46 torpedo.

They were quite a distance from the Falklands/Malvinas islands and mainland Argentina, some 1,400 miles to the east of San Matías Gulf (Golfo San Matías). In the middle of the Atlantic, out of reach of the Argentine Air Force, and very far away from other friendly units. The convoy was moving slowly, but with a long-leg zig-zag, as the doctrine indicated. Humphrey the Wessex and its crew (Sub-Lieutenant Stewart Copper, Lieutenant Chris Parry and Petty Officer Aircrewman David “Fitz” Fitzgerald) were operating at a distance of 12 miles from the HVUs, covering a sector 30 degrees to port and 30 degrees to starboard along the line of advance of the convoy.

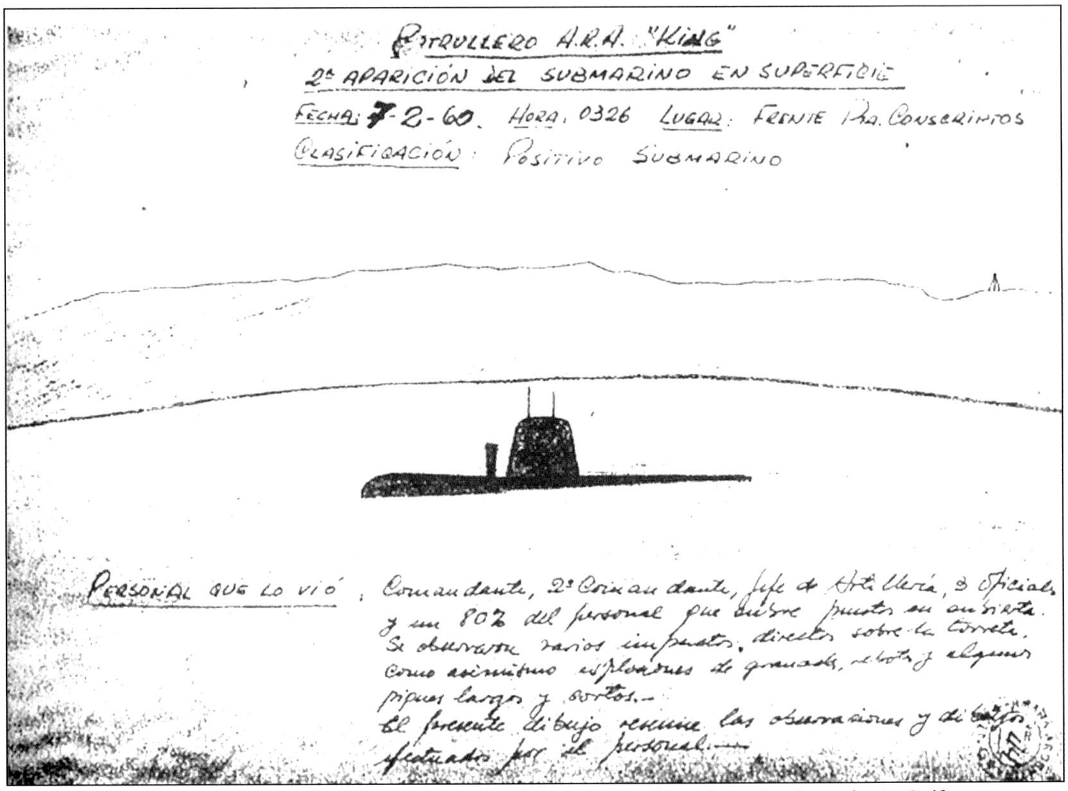

POSITIVO SUBMARINO (CERTSUB). On 7 February 1960, the submarine intruder in Golfo Nuevo was detected on the surface by patrol ship ARA *King*. The *King* engaged the submarine with its 40mm gun and “several direct impacts on the fin were observed.”

Five minutes after taking off, and at 10.5 nautical miles in front of the ships, the helicopter dipped its sonar transducer into the sea to a depth of 180 feet (55 metres) and started transmitting. The active sonar immediately detected a promising contact at 3,000 yards. The Observer, Lieutenant Chris Parry, reported urgently to *Antrim*: “X-Ray, FIVE, Uniform this is Zulu FOUR Foxtrot Track 4140 bearing 145, range 30, heading 090, speed 4, classified POSSUB LOW 2.”

The helicopter then raised its sonar and moved to a position around 1,000 yards in front of the POSSUB. In the dip again, the contact was once again established and was described by the Observer as a “fat sausage-shaped contact, with good definition”. After a prolonged analysis by Lieutenant Parry and Petty Officer Fitzgerald, they ruled out a contact being a whale or other form of marine life and no whale sounds were heard in Passive mode. On the sonar display, it had the right size and shape to be a submarine. This meant that the confidence level was raised to POSSUB HIGH 3, and then POSSUB HIGH 4. Lt Parry communicated back to HMS *Antrim* by radio that he would proceed to drop a Mk 46 torpedo on it.

Once dropped, the torpedo began its zigzag search pattern towards its target at 3,400 yards – but at the end of its run, no explosion was detected. On lowering the sonar transducer once again, which had been raised when the torpedo entered the water so that it did not have any kind of effect on it, the helicopter gained the contact once again. Now, the contact was violently changing speed, up to 28 knots, and depth, coming up and going under the thermal layer. In addition to this, three bubble making decoys were detected.

The contact was maintained for around 50 minutes. Even though, by now, the *Plymouth*’s Wasp was airborne in support, it was not authorised to drop a second torpedo. Humphrey the Wessex needed to return to *Antrim* to refuel and rearm and therefore the contact was lost as the Wasp had no sonar or other means to prosecute the contact.

Contrary to what could be imagined, Lt Parry received a reprimand for wasting a torpedo from *Antrim*’s CO on their return. The ship considered the contact to be nothing more than a whale. According to the crew debrief:

> Although the Command considered this target to be marine life, both the Observer and the Aircrewman (sonar operator) were convinced that a submarine was held during this action. Although intelligence intimated that an Argentine threat was low in this area, the contact gained seemed to fit all the criteria for a submarine. Possibly it was a submarine from another Navy.

The pilot flying the Wessex that day, Sub-Lieutenant Stewart Cooper, also wrote in his diary:

> Found what was thought to be a submarine in afternoon trip. Loosed off a Mk 46 at it. No joy. The ship took no notice and the Captain said it was a whale. I hope it was. The Mk 46 did not explode.
>
> The ‘whale’ which we found was of course a submarine, but the ship wouldn’t tell us that it was because that would have breached security. Quite an interesting situation and a lesson learnt (I hope) – tell the aircrew what you know! After all, whose sub was it?! We did find out later.

The last comment would suggest that Royal Navy’s warship commanders were aware of the presence of submarines of other nations operating in the area but did not necessarily wish to share this information with those tasked with ASW duties.

The Soviet Navy intelligence ship *Zaporozhye* photographed from Type 42 destroyer HMS *Glasgow* ... (Royal Navy)

... and HMS *Glasgow* from *Zaporozhye*. Both photographs were taken near Ascension Island, when *Glasgow* was returning home after sustaining damage from an Argentine Air Force bomb. The bomb´s exit hole is clearly visible just above the waterline. (Soviet Navy)

ACT THREE

Soviet submarines' presence in the South Atlantic

The first Soviet submarine to enter the South Atlantic did so in 1958. This was a Zulu-class boat, according to its NATO reporting name; Project 611 according to its Soviet designation. B-75, commanded by Captain 2nd Rank M.K. Malkova, got to a latitude as far as 1° 50′ South.

Following this first, and almost imperceptible visit, there were almost immediately a series of other missions venturing into the South Atlantic by Soviet submarines. These were as much for scientific purposes as they were military in nature. They carried out experiments to measure the Earth's gravitational fields; salinity of the sea; collation of temperatures, sea currents and other such data that would be useful for future ballistic missile submarine operations in the area, which was considered to possess few anti-submarine defences.

Maybe a few of these submarines were involved in a series of incidents involving the Argentine Navy, never recognised by the USSR, off Patagonia in the southern tip of Argentina. These incidents took place in 1958, 1959 and 1960 and involved a big part of the Argentine Navy against mysterious submerged contacts. On 27 February 1960, a few days after the most serious of these incursions, the US President, Dwight Eisenhower, in the company of the Argentine President, Arturo Frondizi, flew from Mar de Plata to Bariloche, in Patagonia, to take part in an event together.

As noted in the official US minutes of that pleasant meeting between the two leaders, they chatted about the submarines. And Frondizi gave his opinion about the subject:

> The conversation then turned to the subject of the submarine contacts in Golfo Nuevo. The President asked whether there really had been submarines there. President Frondizi replied that there had. In fact, it was believed that there had been two and possibly a third. In reply to a question by the President (Eisenhower), President Frondizi expressed the belief that they were checking the route around Cape Horn, which the Free World would be forced to use in case of a generalized conflict and in the case of the Panama Canal being rendered unusable, for whatever reason. Likewise, it

In this action, besides being able to confirm, perhaps, the presence of submarines of another nationality in the waters of the South Atlantic, it is clear that the British forces did not neglect its anti-submarine doctrine, despite being far from the Theatre of Operations and operating with very limited resources of two escorts and two helicopters.

Likewise, it is possible to see there was, at times, an appreciable difference of opinion between those on the scene and those onboard ships. This also happened in the Argentine Navy in their anti-submarine operations on 5 May, in the vicinity of the Bahía Camarones. Other than this, if there was a submarine trailing the British convoy, it clearly was not Argentine. None of their submarines were near the convoy.

A Type 21 frigate in the South Atlantic. It is interesting to note that this photograph was taken from a Soviet TU-95RTS ("Bear D") flying from Luanda, Angola. (via Dmitriy Ermolin)

gave the Soviet Union long-range experience for its crews with minimum danger owing to the obsolescent equipment which the Argentines had.

The Soviets maintained the presence of their submarines in the South Atlantic over the years that followed. Evidence of their interest in the region during the Cold War came in the form of the unexpected arrival of a Project AB611 (NATO reporting name: Zulu V-class), at Port Stanley (the capital of the Falklands/Malvinas) in February 1972. This submarine, Hull Number B-73, was obliged to visit this not so friendly port as it had suffered a serious technical breakdown while carrying out research in the area for military purposes.

It should be added that the Soviet submarines not only carried out patrols in these waters, but also used the Drake Passage to transit from their European bases to and from the Pacific. Therefore, it is not a huge leap of imagination to deduce that the South Atlantic was not exactly an unknown area for the Soviet submarine fleet. Likewise, it is not far-fetched to assume that these vessels, with the opportunity to gather a vast amount of invaluable intelligence about one of their principal Cold War adversaries, were covertly operating in and around the area of operations during the time of the conflict between the UK and Argentina.

At the outbreak of events, a conventional Foxtrot-class submarine (Project 641 for the Soviets) was known to be in the South Atlantic and operating out of the port of Luanda in Angola, alongside other Soviet surface units. This submarine, hull number B-826 and named *Yaroslavsky Komsomolets*, was in the area from 23 January until 19 September 1982, at least in the vicinity of the African coast. The presence of any other Soviet submarine in the South Atlantic was never confirmed by the Soviet Navy or its successor.

The first indication that there was another submarine operating in the area came from the US Naval Attaché in Buenos Aires. On 1 April, on the eve of the Argentine landings on the Falklands/Malvinas, he informed his British counterpart, and he in turn informed London; "they have confirmed presence of Soviet submarine, one or more in Falkland Islands". Also, the US Naval Attache was "informed by an Argentine Naval Officer at a cocktail party ... for Admiral Hayward that Soviets have fishing fleet 50 miles off Falkland Islands and that Soviet submarines [are] sitting under fishing fleet". This information was also passed to the British Embassy and then directly to London.

Two weeks later, on the 15th, after an unexplained delay bearing in mind that the Soviet Union was a common enemy for the Western Block, the US Navy relayed its own information about Soviet boats' presence to the Argentine Navy. Likewise, it is useful to note that on the 14 April, the Soviet official newspaper Pravda published an article stating that the Soviet submarines in the area were not a destabilising factor without specifically denying their presence near the disputed islands.

Paradoxically, Admiral Harry D. Train II, SACLANT during the conflict, when asked about the presence of Soviet submarines in the conflict zone, in a conference held in Argentina in November 1986, replied that "I do not think any soviet boat were there. I have to say that, being where I was, I must have known about it". Despite these contradictions, both sides had been able to perceive the presence in the area of submarines belonging to a third-party during the conflict.

An example of this is an incident with a report from 15 April by the British Joint Intelligence Committee (JIC). This report declared that there were no Soviet submarines in the South Atlantic. In a meeting that took place the following day in Northwood, the Royal Navy's operational headquarters strongly disagreed with this claim, indicating "that no one could be that categorical about the absence of Soviet submarines", and finished up with some dismissive comments about the quality of the JIC's appreciation of the situation. The British admirals knew full well that Soviet submarines could be anywhere in the world.

The JIC report had been motivated by the detection, a few days earlier, of a Soviet nuclear-powered submarine, a possible Project 670 *Skat* (a Charlie-class boat, according to its NATO reporting name), that was transiting around the west of the British Isles in a southerly direction. The initial detection of this vessel had been made by HMS *Superb*, which passed the news on to the Nimrods of the RAF. The *Superb* then headed to port with the joke going around the crew that they would enter as HMS *Surprise* – as most of the world's press believed them to be in the seas around the Falklands/Malvinas.

With the crisis over the Falklands/Malvinas building up, this intruder was of interest to the British forces. They were particularly keen to stop it from heading to the South Atlantic, where it might possibly interfere in British operations, or at least to track its movements. Round the clock surveillance missions were mounted to track the submarine as it made its way through the waters of the North Atlantic. This role, at first, lay with the RAF's Nimrod fleet and then passed over "hot" to the US Navy's P-3C Orions.

The presence of the Charlie-class boat and its route to the south caused a large discussion in London about whether the Soviets might become involved in combat operations in the South Atlantic. The same afternoon that the JIC report was published, on the 15 April, and while the submarine was being closely monitored, a British War Cabinet meeting took place. The topics discussed included the rules of engagement for Operation Paraquet (the operation to recover South Georgia), and a short discussion about the possible interference of communist forces.

That night, the Foreign and Commonwealth Office considered that:

> It will be prudent to make an approach in Moscow to warn the Russians to keep their surface vessels and submarines well clear of the South Atlantic area, and of our Maritime Exclusion Zone in particular, to minimize the risk of inadvertent encounters in any naval action that may prove necessary.

As a result of these thoughts and discussions, an encrypted telegram was sent to the British Ambassador to the Soviet Union, Sir Curtis Keeble, requesting that he communicate the following verbatim to the Soviet Government:

> Her Majesty´s Government express the hope that the Soviet Government will draw the appropriate conclusions for its own shipping in the South Atlantic area and will take all necessary precautions to keep well clear, in the interest of avoiding errors, accidents or misunderstandings.

On 17 April, the message was relayed by telephone to the Soviet authorities, who did not make any kind of response to the message other than "received". They then took the opportunity to endorse their view that they considered the war to be an act of British aggression.

In any case, the tension subsided the next morning when a US Navy P-3C Orion aircraft, operating from Rota in Spain, confirmed that the submarine had finally entered the Mediterranean via the Straits of Gibraltar.

The last piece in this jigsaw is the curious case of possible collaboration between the Soviet Union and Argentina. This is the offer made to the *de facto* Argentine President (and member of the Junta), General Leopoldo Fortunato Galtieri for the Soviets to torpedo a British vessel and let the Argentines take the credit for it.

On 9 April, after an eventful journey in which his plane was intercepted by Brazilian fighters, Emilio Aragonés Navarro, the Cuban Ambassador to Argentina, and personal representative of Fidel Castro, arrived back in Argentina. He had been absent for a year following the accusation made by the Argentine Government that the Cubans had financed and supported the left-wing guerrillas that had been operating in Argentina in the previous decade.

The following day, Aragonés Navarro met with Galtieri. After being thanked for their gestures of solidarity, the former indicated that "behind this, there is a willingness to do something that needs to be done.... send a submarine and sink a ship.... or whatever else".

By the 11th, this offer had permeated through to the Argentine press. The *Diarios y Noticias* (DyN) press agency, citing a "reliable diplomatic source" from the Eastern Bloc, intimated that Moscow was prepared to help Argentina in any way possible, not excluding military support, and made it known that there was a Soviet submarine patrolling the waters around the Falklands/Malvinas.

A couple of days later, Galtieri met with General Alexander Haig, the US mediator (Haig was appointed mediator by the US government to end the crisis peacefully – but in the end it didn´t work). He told Haig that:

> The Cubans implied they were speaking on behalf of the Soviets, even hinting that they had offered to sink the British aircraft carrier (with Prince Andrew on board), leaving the British and the world with the impression that an Argentine submarine had done it.

It is entirely possible that General Galtieri was using the offer as leverage with Haig regarding the danger of the escalation of the conflict. Or maybe the Soviet submarines were already in the South Atlantic, waiting for the order to attack. In any case, it could not be ruled out that the mysterious contacts possibly were submarines "from another Navy."

9

"GOD SMILED ON *ALACRITY* THAT NIGHT"

THE *SAN LUIS*: 8 MAY TO THE END OF ITS WAR PATROL

After the hectic events on 1 May, the ARA *San Luis* did not manage to make any further clear sonar contacts. It did have a few scares and made a number of movements from the patrol area MARIA to the area closest and adjacent to the capital of the islands, denominated ISABEL.

Most of the scares came from radar rackets, which happened when the submarine was snorkelling and with masts up. The submariners only had a very basic knowledge of the electronic order of battle and, possibly, some of the emissions detected were from Argentine aircraft or from land-based radar. Also, the ESM equipment of *San Luis* was not modern or useful. Explained by Azcueta:

> The ARUR 10-B and IAG-1 ESM suite only provided an early alarm about the enemy's radar emissions. Its operating characteristics and its bulky set of antennas did not allow (to avoid excessive risk) to carry out an analysis of the signal and scarcely, at some time, it was able to determine the emission´s azimuth. The ARUR 10-B and IAG-1 ESM suite is obsolete.

However, the submarine was not actively being hunted.

One of the orders it received on 2 May required it to change the cipher keys it was using as it was thought that they might have been compromised following the capture of the *Santa Fe* in South Georgia, though in fact, the *Santa Fe*'s crewmembers had burned the cipher book and erased all keys on the crypto machines before disembarking.

As recounted by the submarine's Communications Officer, *Teniente de Fragata* Alejandro Maegli:

> ... it was feared that the keys had fallen into the possession of the enemy. Therefore, to generate keys for each message, which until then had been taken from the extremely secret code book for the submarines, would now be taken from the Operations Manual for the *Salta* Class submarines. All copies of this manual, except for ours, were now in the hands of COFUERSUB. It was a rather cumbersome procedure, but was pretty secure as only ourselves and the submarine command possessed copies of this manual.

Sonar equipment inside ARA *San Luis*. The bearded sonar team member, *Cabo Primero* Oscar Alberto Serrano, looks tired in a pause during the May 1982 operations. The Safare-Crouzet DUUG-1D broadband sonar interceptor console is clearly visible on the bulkhead (top left). (via Daniel Mesa)

COFUERSUB notified the submariners to look for a particular letter, in a particular line and on a particular page of the Operations Manual (there were few Operations Manual and all copies were in Argentina). In this way messages were sent and received. It was an off-the-cuff method that had been come up with, which COFUERSUB thought might not be understood by those on the submarine. But, fortunately, they did. The final message of the verification process of the new system finished with a secret instruction to Azcueta to "give *Teniente* Maegli a double ration of rum". Unfortunately for Maegli, due to the fact the submarine was not carrying any rum, this could not be enacted.

This improvement in the security of the encipher keys gave the *San Luis* a bit of a breather but, even with this new method, British forces continued to intercept and decipher Argentine communications throughout the conflict.

In the final hours of 8 May, the Argentine submarine was trying to identify a faint contact again inside area MARIA, when the sonar operator picked up a strange noise in the stern sector, which was quickly evaluated as a possible torpedo. Trying to avoid the weapon's lock, the submarine was forced to increase speed, to make evasive manoeuvres and to drop countermeasures. Azcueta wrote at the time in the submarine´s diary:

> The sonar hears a loud and sustained noise in the ship's baffles and evaluates it as a possible torpedo. All rudder to port is ordered, maximum speed and to launch two decoys. The submarine reaches 19 knots. After three and a half minutes is ordered to stop the motors and turn to listen again.

Upon regaining the contact, and after sonar ruled out the possibility of marine life producing it, *Capitán* Azcueta concluded it was a possible submarine in approach at 2,500 yards. At 0042 on 9 May he ordered the firing of a Mk 37 mod 3 torpedo (the SST-4 had

Teniente de Fragata Alejandro Maegli (*San Luis´* Communications Officer) at the attack periscope and *Capitán de Fragata* Fernando Azcueta (*San Luis´* Commanding Officer) during the 1982 combat operations. (via Fernando Azcueta)

HMS *Arrow* (F13) as she approaches RFA *Fort Grange* (A385) on 13 June 1982 at 1355z. 824 NAS C Flight was based on this support ship. (John Osmond)

no anti-submarine capability), on a snake search pattern and settings for 120 feet (36.58 metres) max depth search. Maximum time to target was estimated at 10 minutes. The submarine slowly turned towards an escape course after launch. The weapon continued its path and a detonation was heard 16 minutes later on the contact bearing, possibly after the torpedo struck the sea floor. No secondary explosions were detected, and the sonar operators lost the contact after the detonation.

Some hours later, at 0446, *San Luis*' sonar team detected a new contact, that had very similar characteristics to the previous one and was very close to *San Luis*. Azcueta ordered an increase in speed and set course for the enemy: unable to launch a torpedo against a target that close, his idea was to ram it. Seconds before the collision, noises of krill (marine life) were heard by the puzzled sonarmen, and the submarine was then immersed among them. Post event analysis concluded the target of ARA *San Luis´* torpedo was not a submarine. Its commander recorded in the war diary that:

> Reconstructing the different circumstance surrounding the previous event that culminated in the launch of a torpedo.... it is concluded that the first contact must also have been a shoal of krill although for not having been able to enter it, a classification was not achieved.

Of course, none of the three British submarines in theatre were anywhere near the area where the incident took place. In any case, the chances of successfully hitting an alert nuclear-powered submarine were limited. The maximum speed of these vessels was well in excess of that of the Mk 37 mod 3 torpedo fired at it (26 knots maximum). But, as Azcueta recalled: "It's preferable to lose a torpedo than to lose a submarine. It will be necessary, in the future, to increase experience and training by carrying out submarine versus submarine exercises."

Following the scare, the *San Luis* recharged its batteries by snorkelling, also receiving radio traffic from COFUERSUB. Once the batteries were fully charged, the commander decided to return to the seabed. There it sat, at a depth of 82 metres (269 feet), from 0725 until 2130. In the war diary, Azcueta wrote:

> Among the crew, the nervous tension has increased markedly in the last days; the events of the previous day have impacted clearly and evidently on the atmosphere onboard. The news that we received by radio did nothing to improve morale. However, I appreciate the fact that the crew are more focused and settled now that at the beginning.

Late in the afternoon on 10 May, while the ARA *San Luis* was situated in the MARIA patrol area and guarding the entrance to Falkland Sound (Estrecho de San Carlos), a surface contact was detected heading for the Sound. *Capitán* Azcueta, sure it would return, positioned the submarine to wait.

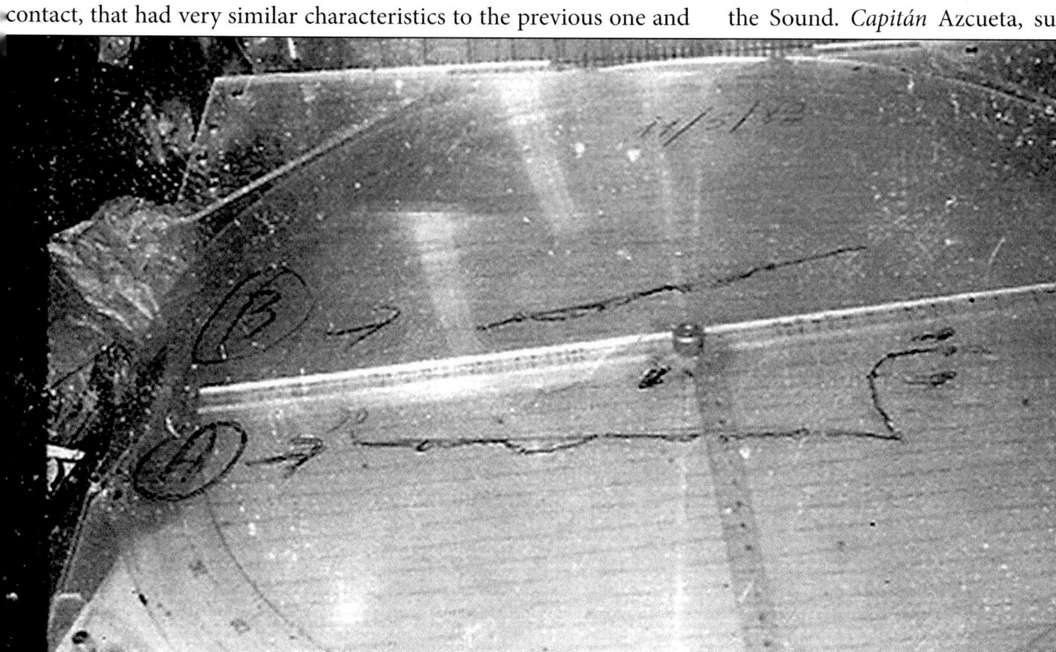

ARA *San Luis´* plot, 11 May 1982. HMS *Arrow* is the target at the top, HMS *Alacrity* at the bottom. The submarine was in between both contacts. (Alejandro Maegli)

The contact was travelling at high speed and the *San Luis* had not been able to get into a position to fire its torpedoes. As he told the crew "it's not a good idea to speed up and cavitate as the sound propagation is very good". At 2330z, they raised the periscope in order to try to see what the target was, but "due to the low light level, it was not possible to see any ship". However, Azcueta wrote in the submarine´s diary, "the radar emissions coming from the target changed to a shorter pulse, consistent with having detected something. Fearing that I have given a radar datum, I will not repeat the observation during the approximation". In

Old Salts Reunited. Commodore Chris J S Craig RN Rtd, HMS *Alacrity* CO (left) and *Capitán de Navío* VGM (RE) Fernando María Azcueta, ARA *San Luis* CO (right) meeting near Portsmouth on July 2019, 37 years after *San Luis* launched a torpedo against *Alacrity*. The author helped to organize this meeting. (via Chris Craig)

other words, the ESM equipment on the submarine had detected a possible counter-detection by the radar on the enemy ship.

It was deemed better to wait for the return of the target. From the experience of 1 May, it was known that the British ships would return to the Carrier Group via the same route.

About 0330 on 11 May, the sonar operators in the sub began to track passively not one but two contacts on their consoles. According to their noise signature, the submarine classified them as two warships, either destroyers or frigates, and began its attack manoeuvre as there were no Argentine ships active in the patrol area, so any contact was assumed hostile. Active sonar in the 6 kHz frequency was detected coming from the targets' bearing.

These targets were the Type 21 frigates HMS *Alacrity* (Commander Chris Craig) and HMS *Arrow* (Commander Paul Bootherstone). They were returning to the Carrier Group, in an anti-submarine formation, at a speed of 22 knots and both towing their torpedo decoys. HMS *Alacrity* had been assigned the dangerous task of transiting Falkland Sound (Estrecho de San Carlos) from south to north to see if it had been mined and also "to attempt to detect and, if possible, disrupt any Argentine re-supply operations". Whilst carrying out these orders no mines were discovered during the journey up the Sound, and indeed none had been placed there by the Argentines. However, Alacrity did come across and sink an Argentine Navy logistics ship, the ARA *Isla de los Estados,* using its 4.5 inch main cannon.

HMS *Arrow* had been handed the task of rendezvousing with *Alacrity* on its exit from the northern end of the Sound, and for the two of them to transit at high speed back to the Carrier Group, making sure that they were back within its air cover umbrella by first light. The two ships would have been very vulnerable to an Argentine air attack if they had not made it back to cover by then.

Prior to the rendezvous with HMS *Alacrity*, while to the north of McBride Head (Península de San Luis), *Arrow* gained a sonar contact at 0217, which it had classified as POSSUB LOW 2, went to Action Stations and passed to an ultra-quiet running state. At 0229, the contact was reclassified as NONSUB, as it was determined that all they had detected had been a rock formation on the seabed. It is entirely possible, from the location of this contact, that the sonar operators had detected the *San Luis*, but did not realise this.

Returning to the Carrier Battle Group at high speed rendered their sonar equipment completely deaf to the menace of the submarine. The *San Luis* was moving slowly underwater and approached within 8,000 yards of the southernmost ship; HMS *Alacrity*.

According to Azcueta:

> I did not raise the periscope as it was dark. The firing conditions were excellent, just like we were in a test range: close distance and excellent target data. I brought the submarine to a halt so that we would not overrun the guiding wire and to stop our relative movement in order to facilitate the guidance of the torpedo. The firing was carried out using information gained from the sonar in very good sonar conditions. There was nothing else to do, at least that I could think of. The torpedo would be fired at the ship that was sailing along the coast, which was believed to be *Alacrity*. *Arrow* was to my starboard.

Capitán de Fragata Fernando Azcueta talks to *San Luis'* crew, informing them that the submarine is now heading back to port. (via Daniel Mesa)

The morning after the war. ARA *San Luis* and part of its crew in Puerto Belgrano Naval Base, the day after the arrival, the submarine having arrived late at night. In the background, is the aircraft carrier ARA *25 de Mayo*. (via Daniel Mesa)

Azcueta ordered "Fire number one torpedo tube" at 0442. The manually calculated fire control solution included the information that the target bearing was 225° and it was heading east (090°) at 18 knots (R.P.M. count was 170). Angle on the Bow was starboard 40°. *San Luis'* speed was only four knots. However, there was a misfire. The torpedo, an SST-4, did not leave the tube.

A couple of minutes later, the necessary time to prepare a new launching, because according to Argentine Navy doctrine only one torpedo tube was flooded at a time, with the target now at an estimated distance of 5,200 yards, Azcueta again ordered a weapon to be fired. This time, another of the problematic SST-4s successfully swam out of torpedo tube eight. It was on a slow-speed setting, in passive mode and in snake search pattern.

The torpedo was launched at an almost optimal distance and, as the target was between the coast and the submarine, the estimated distance to the target could not have been too inaccurate. In order to be able to calculate a correct firing solution for a torpedo, it is necessary to establish, as accurately as possible, a target's range, bearing, course and speed. In this case, at least three of the variables were almost exact.

The SST-4 headed away from the submarine on a course of 180° bearing and everything seemed to be working correctly. When it had cleared the submarine, the torpedo was commanded to run at high-speed and the order was accepted by the torpedo. After this, a small course correction was directed to the weapon and, as had happened on 1 May, at three minutes into its run the lost guidance wire signal flashed up on the console and the noise of the remains of the wire were heard to strike the submarine. At the moment the wire was lost, the torpedo had not yet acquired a target with its own sonar. The torpedo, however, kept going. Three minutes later, a metallic noise was heard from the torpedo's bearing.

Azcueta order another torpedo to be ready, but this was aborted after a sound that was considered to be a possible enemy torpedo on the starboard side was picked up. Later, it was realised that this noise was the sound of the number three torpedo tube being flooded prior to the launch. Azcueta was later criticised by the Argentine High Command for his use of the SST-4s instead of the Mk 37 torpedoes and, also for not firing more than one Mk 37 torpedo simultaneously. However, he maintains that:

> Our doctrine did not include the use of a salvo of acoustic torpedoes due to the interferences that would be generated between them. Besides, a single SST-4 acoustically scans the area in front of it far better than a Mk 37 and can be controlled from the submarine. The Mk 37 is essentially an anti-submarine weapon and is slow and noisy. It should only be deployed against a surface target as a self-defence measure. The reason for this is that they are only suitable for using against targets that are moving under 21 knots. Both targets, that night, were travelling at that speed or higher which would have meant that the weapon would have been used at the limit of, or outside, of its parameters. Using a Mk 37s was nonsensical. And the SST-4 had not fully demonstrated yet their poor performance.

After the attempted attack, when HMS *Arrow* recovered their Type 182 torpedo decoy, it was discovered to have been badly damaged. At the time, it was thought that it must have hit some submerged rock formation or even the seabed. However, it is conceivable that the damage might have been caused by the lost Argentine torpedo that changed its course and, finally, did not explode.

The *San Luis*' crew were expecting for there to be a vigorous anti-submarine response to their attack, as they had witnessed on 1 May. In the words of *Cabo* Alberto Poskin, once again: "we were thinking… okay, we are finished…now they (the British) will start their counter-attack". But nothing happened. Because of the target's speed and position, and assuming incorrectly that both ships would have been alerted to their attack, Azcueta broke off the engagement. He was also upset by the ineffectiveness of the weapon system: "The launch was made at a very short distance and in perfect kinematic conditions. The failure of that launch led me to the conclusion that the weapon system was not reliable."

However, the attack went unnoticed by the British warships, which arrived safely back at the Carrier Battle Group at approximately 1100. In fact, Commander Chris Craig, HMS *Alacrity*'s CO, only learned of the attempted attack a year later, when he received a copy of the combat report that had been written by Azcueta. According to Commander Craig:

> I had no reason to doubt his word. His timing and position fitted our departure precisely. I had elected to return at our best speed, conducting evasive steering and towing our torpedo decoys astern. I had been well aware that our high speed precluded us detecting anything on sonar, but that was another balancing of risk: to have been still short of Task Force air cover at first light could have proved disastrous. It appeared that God smiled on *Alacrity* that night.

A few hours later, at 0931, a disheartened ARA *San Luis* skipper broke radio silence and transmitted the following message to COFUERSUB:

> AT ENSENADA DEL NORTE POSITION, I HAVE ATTACKED TWO DD/FF. 6 KHZ SONARS, VERY GOOD DATA AND LAUNCH POSITION. FIRST TORPEDO FIRED IN EMERGENCY MODE, GUIDANCE WIRE WAS LOST, NO IMPACT. LAUNCH ON SECOND TARGET ABORTED. I CONSIDER WEAPON SYSTEM UNRELIABLE. OWN POSITION KNOWN BY THE ENEMY.

After receiving the message, COFUERSUB ordered the submarine to return to port. The message was received and, at 2100, the submarine headed towards mainland Argentina.

According to *San Luis´* pilot, *Teniente de Corbeta* Luis Seghezzi:

> In a signal that was received in the next snorkelling period, COFUERSUB ordered us to return to port, following a route contained in the signal. The ordered course to return to Puerto Belgrano was not a direct one. It opened towards the east, following an arc that took us into deep waters in the Atlantic. I seem to remember that at some spots along the course we would find fishing vessels that could camouflage our noise.

Finally, after bypassing HMS *Valiant* and on 19 May, after 39 days on patrol (864 hours submerged), ARA *San Luis* arrived at Puerto Belgrano Naval Base. Although the crew and dockyard workers then swarmed all over the submarine in an attempt to make repairs and prepare it for another patrol, it was not to be. The Argentine forces on the islands surrendered less than a month later, before repairs had been completed.

10
THE THREAT LESSENS AND, FINALLY, THE WAR ENDS

Following the seizure of the ARA *Santa Fe*; with the confirmation that the ARA *Santiago del Estero* was hiding in Puerto Belgrano and the news of the return to port of the ARA *San Luis*, the anti-submarine anxiety of the Royal Navy diminished considerably. The only uncertainty, at times, was the location of the ARA *Salta*. However, thanks to communications intercepts, the Royal Navy was fully aware of the constant problems this submarine was suffering.

At the time of Operation Sutton (the British landing in San Carlos) Argentine submarines were not such a big concern in the grand scheme of things. The only ASW operations in support of the landings on 21 May was a MAD search of the area by helicopters of 826 NAS prior to the entry of the landing ships through the strait, in addition to an ASW patrol carried out by HMS *Yarmouth*.

Type 22 frigate HMS *Broadsword* assumed the duties of Anti-Submarine and Surface Warfare Coordinator in San Carlos Water, and planned some ASW sweeps by surface units, but the daylight attacks by the Argentine aircraft forced the frigate to take up an Anti-Air Warfare defence position, as directed by HMS *Antrim* (the AAW Coordinator). Only a detachment of four 826 NAS Sea Kings operating from RFA *Fort Austin* were left to cover the submarine threat. On 23 May, land forces reported a submarine in Grantham Sound (Bahía de Ruiz Puente) and HMS *Broadsword*, assisted by a Sea King, investigated the dubious contact. Nothing was found.

From this point forward, the anti-submarine operations were reduced but never fully abandoned and only sporadic contacts were gained. As explained by the CO of one of the escorts: "It became clear that the submarine threat was minimal and thereafter little more that lip service was paid to it as HVUs were despatched on a regular basis in an out the Area of Operations, often with scanty ASW escort."

In fact, the four 826 NAS Sea Kings operating from RFA *Fort Austin*, as well as the two Sea Kings belonging to A Flight, 824 NAS, were detached to San Carlos on 3 June to support the logistic tail of the land forces. This change from their main mission, in light of the low level of anti-submarine threat, lasted through to 7 June.

The Argentine Air Force and Naval Air Arm reacted swiftly to the landings. The Argentine naval fleet, however, remained either in port or in coastal waters having not found a counter to the British submarine threat. In spite of sinking and damaging various British ships, the Argentines were unable to stop the British forces consolidating the beachhead.

The most notable incident in this stage of the war happened at 0045 on the 2 June. While operating as part of the Carrier Battle Group, the

On 25 May 1982, a bomb dropped by an Argentine Air Force A-4B bounced off the water through the starboard quarter of HMS *Broadsword*, emerging through the flight deck and over the side, taking the nose of Lynx XZ729 with it, as well as breaking the Mk 44 torpedo which was fitted to the starboard side. The helicopter MAD, apparently undamaged, is also clearly visible in this photograph. (MoD)

Type 42 destroyer HMS *Cardiff* gained an intermittent sonar contact in the location of 51° 28.60'S 55 26.12'W. This was classified as a POSSUB LOW 2 and was lost around 25 minutes later. The contact was regained at 0120. This time, *Cardiff* had the Type 82 destroyer HMS *Bristol* for company, as well as two ASW Sea Kings from 826 NAS. The contact was classified as POSSUB HIGH 3 at 2,400 yards. At this point, *Cardiff* launched a Mk 46 torpedo. Forty-five seconds after being launched, and having run about 1,000 yards, the torpedo exploded violently. According to Able Seaman Kenneth Griffiths, a radar operator on board the *Cardiff*:

> When I entered for my watch, I became aware that the sonar guys seemed to be way more alert than normal and there were some raised voices around the Principle Warfare Officer's (PWO) plot. Very soon after I had settled at my position the ship started manoeuvring in ever increasing steepening turns, then soon after that there was an increase in speed and the PWO shouted abruptly "Action STWS". One of the guys who we called 'Pigsy' put his life jacket on and we all laughed energetically. *Cardiff* raced towards a contact ahead of us and fired a torpedo, the feeling in the operations room was calm, I think this was due to the fact that we had not long been in position and also, I personally did not think there was a submarine there! It seemed only a matter of a minute or so after it launched, the torpedo exploded, the violent shock of the explosion inside *Cardiff* was something we had not anticipated at all, it actually felt like it had exploded close under the ship...very close. After the huge explosion, the captain stood up, took his headset off and with a huge silly grin on his face declared "I am going to the bridge to smell for diesel".

After the explosion, the contact was lost once again. It was finally picked up again at 0225 and it was held for a further twenty minutes by *Cardiff* until it was finally lost when the ship left the search area. The two Sea Kings remained there for a short time more without any further contact.

It was just a question of time before the capital of the islands fell on 14 June. The anti-submarine war continued until that day, and long after. After all, nobody could be exactly sure where a submarine was once it had left its port.

It is evident that the British forces were effective in the anti-submarine war, albeit with an amount of luck given the material condition and problems suffered by the Argentine submarines and their torpedoes. As the commander of HMS *Plymouth* reflected:

> In retrospect the inability of the 209s to make any impact on our force almost certainly owes more to their inability to master the complexities of their systems than to a significant advance in our ability to deal with such quiet and potent submarines. Our good fortune in this aspect of the operation was one of the most significant factors in ensuring our subsequent victory so speedily and at such low cost.

It is rather ironic that by the time the British anti-submarine professionals had become fully accustomed to the unique conditions of the South Atlantic and the number of false alarms noticeably decreased, the Argentine submarines had already returned definitively to their home port.

The British anti-submarine forces achieved their task – no British ship was sunk by an Argentine submarine: the satisfaction of a job well

A Sea King HAS.5 of 820 NAS operating from San Carlos forward operating base, around 10 June 1982. The Squadron deliberately left the small airframe serial number on the tail pylon white to help quickly tell the aircraft apart. (Steve George)

done for the British airmen and sailors. It cannot be understood that they have not had the full recognition they really deserve.

However, some sailors received well deserved medals for their war against the Argentine submarines. Among others, Commodore Sam Dunlop (CO RFA *Fort Austin* and the Senior Officer of the Royal Fleet Auxiliary) received the Distinguished Service Order (DSO) for his ASW effort in San Carlos Waters during the landing phase.

Captain John Francis Coward (CO HMS *Brilliant*), Captain Brian Gilmore Young (CO HMS *Antrim*), Lieutenant Commander Ian Stanley (CO *Antrim*´s flight) and Lieutenant Commander John Anthony Ellerbeck (CO HMS *Endurance*´s flight) also received the DSO, partly for his actions against the *Santa Fe*.

Lieutenant Commander Ralph John Wykes-Sneyd (CO 820 NAS) received the Air Force Cross (AFC), for his "personal qualities of cool determination and resolution in preventing submarine attack". Another AFC was for the commander officer of the sister squadron (826 NAS), Lieutenant Commander Douglas John Smiley Squier, who "led his men to provide the necessary anti-submarine defence and surface warning for the Carrier so that the operation could continue".

For their part, the small Argentine submarine force fulfilled, at least partially, their given mission to "disrupt the enemy Expeditionary Force." As explained by the US Navy Admiral Harry D. Train II in his post-war analysis:

> A small force of Argentine diesel electric submarines created enormous concern for the British. It dictated, at least as much as did the air threat, the conduct of British naval operations and caused the expenditure of a vast supply of anti-submarine warfare weapons. Virtually every anti-submarine weapon in the Task Force was expended on false submarine contacts.

But for some people, the mission was not even partially completed. COFUERSUB, with the war having finished, announced that it would not be awarding "the Honour of Valour in Combat" to the standard of the *San Luis* as this implied an outstanding participation for a unit in a conflict.

As its justification, it was stated that: "It is considered that the lack of results due to defects in its weapons systems during its engagements with the enemy constitutes a determining limitation with regard to the decision not to award the distinction". However, it also stated that "the exemplary behaviour of the crew during direct contact with the enemy should be highlighted.

Obviously, nobody in the crew of the *San Luis* liked this. After all, the commander of the submarine force was directly responsible for the faults in the systems and torpedoes. Nevertheless, this view was not shared by the higher command and, finally, the *San Luis* received the "Honour of Valour in Combat" unit citation. At the end of the day, the efforts of the submarine and its crew had finally been recognised.

Ironically, Azcueta never received an award for his leadership under fire. *Cabo Segundo* "Chacho" Felman and the other six members of the ad-hoc fire team of the *Santa Fe*, including the wounded *Cabo* Macías, received the *"Honor al Valor en Combate"* medal, for their "courage and dare while fighting to repel the attack of helicopters to the submarine, regardless of the risk of their own lives, using automatic weapons and with little protection." Submarine ARA *Santa Fe* was only recognised for taking part in the combat operations.

On the other hand, it's worth considering that the Royal Navy also suffered from many of the issues that had plagued the Argentine Navy: doubt over contacts; lack of knowledge of the enemy's equipment; limited reliability of some weapons; a scarcity of information for further analysis and a long list of etcetera.

However, it should be added that the Royal Navy anti-submarine effort was different to that of the Argentine Navy in several aspects.

- The first of these would be the use of active sonar almost exclusively for anti-submarine operations. This was because it was thought to be almost impossible to detect a relatively small modern conventional submarine, such as the *San Luis*, with passive sonar. The Argentine Navy, on the contrary, vetoed the use of active sonar and concentrated on passive listening whether by ship, submarine or aircraft, in order not to alert British submarines with the "ping" of their sonar.
- The second difference was that the Argentine Navy only used a limited number of anti-submarine weapons, launching just a handful of them. The Royal Navy, however, was very liberal in the use of these weapons, even in conditions in which normal doctrine would not permit their use; whether for the classification of a difficult contact or with the aim of destroying a submerged enemy vessel.
- Finally, there was the conviction of the Argentine naval forces, or at least some of its commanding officers, that it was very difficult to detect a British nuclear-powered submarine unless they exposed their masts above the surface. The British forces, faced with the difficulty of detecting an Argentine submarine by using sonar, maximised the recommendations to detect one when it transmitted to its base or made any kind of electro-magnetic emission.

Although both navies started out with a similar doctrine, the Argentine Navy Task Force 79.1 only carried out an extended organised anti-submarine operation while operating in shallow waters for a limited time and with scant resources and weapons as, for example, it possessed just two ASW capable Sea King helicopters.

The Royal Navy, for its part, made a huge anti-submarine effort in deep and shallow waters over a prolonged period, counting on a flawless logistics train which kept its magazines full.

The most important lesson from the conflict is that anti-submarine warfare is an extremely complex and costly affair. It is necessary to have modern equipment and well-trained crews in order to get results, and even with all these resources, may only obtain limited gains.

But, again, the sinking of an enemy submarine is nothing more than a bonus.

References and sources

Documents, UK National Archives / MoD:

820 NAS Report of Proceedings (DEFE 69-838)

824 NAS A Flight Report of Proceedings (Navy Command FOI Section – request-356002-20a21ffb)

Anti-Submarine Warfare (AIR 8-3282)

Balance of Fighting Capability ARA vs RN (DEFE 69-1138)

CTG 317.8 Operation Corporate War Diary (ADM 202-892 and ADM 202-893)

Escorts – Report of Proceedings (DEFE 69-985)

Flag Officer Submarines – Report of Proceedings (DEFE 69/846)

HMS *Antrim* Report of Proceedings (Naval Service FOI Coordination Cell – request 13-03-2006-172157-025)

HMS *Antrim* – Flight Report (DEFE 69-818)

HMS *Arrow* Report of Proceedings (Naval Service FOI Coordination Cell – request 22-01-2009-111725-07)

HMS *Brilliant* – Flight Report (DEFE 69-823)

HMS *Broadsword* – Flight Report (DEFE 69-824)

HMS *Conqueror* Report of Proceedings (Naval Service FOI Coordination Cell – request 08-07-2010-112201-003)

HMS *Invincible* Falklands Islands Campaign Diary (DEFE 69/844)

HMS *Plymouth* – Flight Report (DEFE 69-841)

HMS *Spartan* Report of Proceedings (Naval Service FOI Coordination Cell – requests 16-09-2008-071600-002 and 25-07-2011-105719-003)

HMS *Splendid* Report of Proceedings (Naval Service FOI Coordination Cell – requests 16-09-2008-071600-002 and 25-07-2011-105719-003)

HMS *Valiant* Report of Proceedings (Naval Service FOI Coordination Cell – request 10-12-2010-101254-002)

Lessons Learned – Anti Submarine Warfare (DEFE 69-1086)

Summary of Naval Aircraft Flying Operations Accidents & Statistics (ADM 202-938)

Documents, Argentine Navy Archives:

Capitán de Fragata Azcueta (Former Commander submarine ARA *San Luis*) Interview (COAC Archive – Box MLV084)

Former Commander of the ARA *Santa Fe* Bicain – Interview (COAC Archive – Box MLV084)

Chronological History of Operations – COFUERSUB (COAC Archive – Box MLV025)

Problems with the torpedo tubes on ARA *Salta* class submarine (COAC Archive – Box MLV037)

COFUERSUB Report, Folders 14, 15 and 16 (COAC Archive – Boxes MLV050 and MLV051)

Report of operations submarine ARA *San Luis* (COAC Archive – Box MLV025)

Books/Articles:

Anaya, Jorge, "Malvinas: la guerra justa. Pormenores de la crisis argentino-británica de 1982", *Boletín del Centro Naval n°834*, pp. 263-300.

Barker, Nick, *Beyond Endurance: An Epic of Whitehall and the South Atlantic Conflict.* (South Yorkshire: Pen & Sword, 2001)

Blackman, Tony and Kennedy, Joe, *Nimrod Boys: True Tales from the Operators of the RAF´s Cold War Trailblazer*. (London: Grub Street, 2018)

Bóveda, Jorge, *Malvinas. La odisea del submarino Santa Fe.* (Buenos Aires: Instituto de Publicaciones Navales, 2007)

Bóveda, Jorge, "El secreto del ARA *Salta*", *Boletín del Centro Naval n°833*, pp. 169-176.

Brown, David, *The Royal Navy and the Falklands War.* (London: Arrow Edition, 1989)

Chartres, John, *Westland Sea King.* (London: I Allan, 1984)

Cooper, Stewart, *My Falklands Diary.* (Ebook: Lulu.com, 2007)

Craig, Chris, *Call for fire.* (London: John Murray Ed, 1995)

Fernández Diaz, Jorge, "Viaje al fondo de los mares del Sur", *Diario La Nación*, 22 August 2009.

Friedman, Norman, *The Naval Institute Guide to World Naval Weapons Systems 1991/92.* (Annapolis: Naval Institute Press, 1992)

Inskip, Ian, *Ordeal by Exocet: HMS Glamorgan and the Falklands War 1982.* (South Yorkshire: Frontline Books, 2012)

Jeram-Croft, Larry and Martin, Terry, *The Royal Navy Wasp. An Operational & Retirement History.* (South Yorkshire: Pen & Sword, 2018)

Jones, B, "820 Naval Air Squadron in Operation Corporate", *The Naval Review* (1983), pp. 179-181.

Hill, John Richard, *Anti-Submarine Warfare* 2nd *Edition.* (Annapolis: Naval Institute Press, 1984)

Jinks, James, and Hennessy, Peter, *The Silent Deep. The Royal Navy Submarine Service Since 1945.* (London: Penguin Books, 2015)

Lombardo, Juan José, *Malvinas: Errores, Anécdotas y Reflexiones.* (unpublished)

Mayorga, Horacio A, *No vencidos.* (Buenos Aires: Planeta, 1998).

McManners, Hugh, *Forgotten Voices of the Falklands: The Real Story of the Falklands War,* (London: Ebury Press, 2008).

Parry, Chris, *Down South. A Falklands War Diary.* (London: Viking Press, 2012)

Perowne, James, "The submarine and the operational level", *The Naval Review* (1996), pp. 276.

Ring, Jim, *We Come Unseen. The Untold Story of Britain's Cold War Submariners* (London: John Murray Ed, 2001).

Sciaroni, Mariano with Gillis, J. Matthew, "Almost Successful", *Submarine Almanac 2008*, pp. 19-28.

Seghezzi, Luis, *Vivencias de Luis V. Seghezzi a bordo del Submarino ARA* San Luis *en Malvinas.* (unpublished)

Winton, John, *Signals from the Falklands.* (London: Pen & Sword, 1997)

Woodward, J F, and Robinson P, *One Hundred Days.* (London: Harper Collins Publishers, 2012)

ABOUT THE AUTHORS

Mariano Sciaroni graduated as a lawyer, has a Master's Degree in Strategy and Geopolitics, and a postgraduate qualification in contemporary military history from the Argentine Army's Military Academy. He is currently working as a specialist in insurance and commercial law and lectures in procedural law at the Law Faculty of the Universidad Catolica Argentina. Living with his wife and three children in Buenos Aires, he is a member of the Argentine Institute of Military History and a Sub-Lieutenant in the Argentine Army Reserve. He has written two books and dozens of articles on the military history of Argentina that have been published in Argentina, the United States, Germany, and Russia. This is his second instalment for Helion's @War series.

Andy Smith is from the United Kingdom and has spent the last ten years in intensive research about naval operations during the Falklands War. He has helped multiple Argentine historians of this conflict, organised a highly successful reunion of veterans from both sides, and also put in touch individual veterans with their former enemy. After working and studying in Spain and graduating in Business and Spanish at a university in the UK, he entered a career in marketing, and currently lives in Budapest in Hungary, where he teaches English. He is currently working on multiple projects about the Falklands War, and this is his first instalment for Helion's @War series.